THE GUIDE TO REFORM
Johnny Munkhammar

the
GUIDE
to
REFORM

Johnny Munkhammar

TIMBRO

This book is published by Timbro in association with the Institute of Economic Affairs (IEA).

Since 1978 Timbro has advocated free markets, free trade and free societies.
Timbro incubates the ideas that influence opinion, shape policy and guide enterprise.
Timbro is based in Stockholm, Sweden. For more information, please refer to our website,
<www.timbro.com>.

Founded in 1955, the mission of the IEA is to improve understanding of the fundamental
institutions of a free society by analysing and expounding the role of markets in solving
economic and social problems. It achieves its mission through a wide-ranging publication
and events programme. For further details, visit the IEA's website <www.iea.org.uk>.

Cover design: Helena Ullstrand, Copine Design, Stockholm

Typeset by Original Et AB, Stockholm

Printed and bound by Brommatryck&Brolins AB, Stockholm 2007

ISBN 978-0-255-36618-2

For Rebecka

TABLE OF CONTENTS

ACKNOWLEDGEMENTS

I HAVE STUDIED ISSUES OF reform for a long time. Why reforms are needed, which reforms are important, how some reforms fail—and how they take place. I have also experienced many circumstances in which both problems and opportunities related to reform arise. Fortunately, this has provided me with numerous good friends and colleagues in many countries who are experts on different aspects of this topic. This informal network of people, and their combined experience, has been of great importance to me in the work with this book.

This book is very far from a one-man project, and there have been many different kinds of supporters. First, I would like to thank my colleagues at Timbro for all the input, great efforts and positive attitude—and the Institute of Economic Affairs for their support and professionalism.

Second, I would also especially like to thank Katinka Barysch, John Blundell, Philip Booth, Pontus Braunerhjelm, Odd Eiken, Fredrik Erixon, Kasper Elbjörn, Shane Frith, Stefan Fölster, Hannes Gissurarsson, Andrew Haldenby, David Henderson, Greg McIvor, Richard Jackson, Lars Jonung, Tim Kane, Nils Karlson, Roger Kerr, Dick Kling, PJ Anders Linder, Greg Lindsay, Joakim Munkhammar, Adam Myers, Johan Norberg, Andrew Norton, John Peet, Maria Rankka, Tino Sanandaji, Fredrik Segerfeldt, Rok Spruk, Urban Strandberg,

Jesper Strömbäck, Fabian Wallen, Cathy Windels and Anders Åslund for their advice, comments, discussions, constructive criticism or other forms of co-operation.

Third, thanks to The Economist, Google and the IDEAS database for existing and thus providing indispensable sources of intriguing analyses and information.

Last, but far from least, my everlasting thanks to my wife Linda, the best and most beautiful woman in the world, and to my great inspiration and source of energy, our daughter Rebecka.

Any errors in the book are of course entirely my own responsibility.

Stockholm November 2007
Johnny Munkhammar

PROLOGUE

THE PRIME MINISTER WAS SWEATING slightly. He hoped it would not be visible to the delegates, or at least that they would think it was due to the strong lights. As he looked down at his hand, holding all the papers for his upcoming speech, he could see a tremble.

He was in his mid-fifties and had been chairman of the party and prime minister for eight years. A long time by any measure, and he was proud of the achievement. He had two election victories behind him, though the last one with a narrow margin.

In the last few decades he had given more speeches than he could remember. All the way from the joining the party's youth organisation to entering parliament and finally becoming prime minister, he had been considered an eloquent speaker. He knew this and had an impressive air of self-confidence. But his nerves seemed to betray him this time.

"Confidence," he thought. "Confidence and boldness! Our country is great, not least thanks to this party. We have always taken our responsibility for the future. Change and adopting new ideas are not strange to us. This is the way ahead—the delegates will know it." He repeated the words to himself, though without feeling convinced.

He was the prime minister of a medium-sized European country which was held in high regard internationally, and he was proud to represent it. People associated the country with quality, a fascinating history and sporting prowess. It was also a rather wealthy nation, having once showed the way for others in making the leap from agriculture to industry.

The Labour party, which he led, had been in government for most of the time since World War II. Sometimes it ruled in coalition with a smaller party to ensure a majority in parliament, since the electoral system was based on proportional representation. In its own self-image, the prime minister's party was closely associated with the country's historic successes.

A welfare state had been introduced in this country, as in other parts of the developed world, in the decades after World War II. The size of the state—in terms of taxes, regulations, social security and public welfare services—had doubled several times. All of it was done in the name of social justice.

The Labour party had played the main role, though in fact the other leading party, the Christian Democrats, had supported most of the measures. The original intention had been to expand the size of the state even more, but in the 1980s the trend stopped and in the 1990s the Labour party dropped its socialist ideas. Since then, the emphasis had mostly been on preserving the status quo and achieving consensus.

"I got into politics to make a difference, to improve things, to make a mark on history," the prime minister told himself. He had asked to be alone before his speech at the annual party conference. In the small backstage room, he felt very lonely.

There were real problems in his country. It offered little comfort that many neighbouring countries shared them and sometimes were worse off. And he knew that the recent upturn in the business cycle was temporary. Many people were excluded from society; they had no jobs or opportunities but instead were dependent on the state. Crime was up, incomes were down and health care and schools had persistent problems.

This had been visible in the statistics for some time, and in the past few years the media had homed in on the issues. The public was concerned.

"It's not just economics or politics," he thought. "It's about society changing in numerous respects, in daily life. The world is so close. We don't produce what we did. The population is ageing. Technology makes old solutions obsolete and creates new opportunities. Our public institutions, systems and policies have not kept up."

He had really enjoyed the increasing international dimension in his daily life: meeting other political leaders, having discussions and making an impact. It had increased his popularity at home. But he was highly aware that the degree of impact was dependent on his country's success. In the end, continued decline would mean insignificance. Achieving results in politics, after all, was a result of powerful bargaining.

Economists and businessmen had criticised him for as long as he could remember. It was fairly obvious to them what needed to be done to solve the country's problems. Yet, in their view, the government did nothing. The economists did not think the government listened. And the businessmen often said they would soon be out of business if they refused to act when their companies faced the kind of challenges facing the country.

"We may have made mistakes but nobody could have acted much differently and we are definitely the ones to launch solutions today," the prime minister repeated. "No party for the future can just relax and live off the success of the past. There is now an opportunity for change that we didn't have before."

In fact, his government had launched several reforms. For example, it had deregulated the telecoms market, and the average cost of a one-minute phone call had dropped by 70 per cent in just a few years. This was a small but clear improvement, especially beneficial for ordinary people. But everyone soon got used to it, forgetting how expensive phone calls used to be and never thanking the government or supporting further reform.

The prime minister had always relished the debate between the political parties. But he had been slightly uncomfortable with all the independent voices: academics, editorial writers, think-tanks and businessmen. They were too radical and impatient. But he knew (though he kept it to himself) that without them there would have been little pressure for change and very few proposals for reform.

The annual party conference gathered all the leading lights of the party, some 400 people in all. There were speeches, debates and policy decisions. And any decision, of course, had to be obeyed by the party leadership and hence also by the government. The conference had been preceded by intense media speculation and rumours about drastic changes of policy in a free-market direction. Support for the Labour party was falling in the opinion polls.

The mere rumours about a policy shift had started an intense political spin:

* Representatives of the more traditional wing of the party, who wanted to take over, said that any neo-liberal ideas had to be dismissed.
* A television news programme calculated how much an ordinary family would lose if, as rumours claimed, the government cut sickness, unemployment and early retirement benefits.
* The trade unions, whose extensive economic and societal influence was underpinned by the institutions and regulations of the current order, hinted at withdrawing their support for the party if it deregulated the labour market.
* A number of doctors working in public health care wrote an op-ed about how privatisation and the profit motive would destroy health care provision.
* The leading leftist newspaper ran an editorial about the tragedy of the coming historic break with the most successful model the world had ever known.
* Leading civil servants, who feared cuts in public administration, provided anonymous quotes to the media about possible administrative chaos.
* A self-appointed spokesperson for the early retired urged the government not to abandon the weakest members of society with cuts in social security.
* A state-funded research institute provided a number of statistics showing how income inequality increased in countries that implemented free-market reforms.
* The Christian Democrats accused the government of failure and promised to work for a more "social agenda" if given the chance.
* The Communist party, gaining in the polls, said the country's problems were the result of too much free-market capitalism, not too little.

* A movement for "international solidarity and justice" hinted that the prime minister was in the pocket of capitalists and was copying the model of the "socially unjust" United States.
* A wealthy investment banker, deeply resented by most people for his arrogance, said that finally the prime minister seemed to be doing something right.

The prime minister paced across the room. He had not made a single comment to the media; the speech would be his reply. "Dozens of research publications have shown why we have problems and what we can do to solve them. Many countries have also carried out reforms successfully," he said. "People see this; we will have their support."

He knew the government had really waited a bit too long and feared riots in at least one of the bigger cities if some reforms were postponed. Naturally, such an event could be blamed on others, though this would be a cynical, and above all short-sighted, tactic.

It had been hard for the prime minister to rethink parts of what he had learnt since he was a teenager. The social model actually produced some rather anti-social results. Many state interventions create problems, and indeed in a globalised world of rapid change, they protect the old and block the new. They hamper creation, entrepreneurship and work. Decades in politics had shown him that many policies were launched simply to appease special interests, not to benefit society as a whole.

He had been genuinely surprised to see what had happened in countries that actually carried out free-market reforms. Growth, incomes and employment went up, poverty went down and welfare services improved. Government had an important role in society, but it had also been damaging in the past—and that role had to change.

"This is not a matter of ideology," he thought. "It is a matter of facts and reality. I will always believe in the value of opportunity for all, but we need other policies to succeed. When ordinary people make efforts to improve their lives and futures they have to be rewarded, not punished. That is social justice for tomorrow," he suddenly said out loud.

The clock on the wall said five minutes to twelve. "Symbolic," he thought. The government may have waited to take this step, but there was still time and the new policy proposals were well prepared. Others had paved the way in the public debate for years. He felt that any initial resistance would fade quickly. Once changes were made, nobody would want to return to the old society.

The next election was three years away and the prime minister knew that if the reforms had enough time to show positive results, they would meet with most people's approval. He would be a hero, the man who initiated an enduring new wave of national success. But he and his party had to deliver on the entire process, from identifying ideas and shaping proposals to presenting, defending and implementing them—at the right time and in the right order.

An orchestra had started playing in the conference hall. In a matter of minutes, he would enter and there would be standing ovations. Then what? His speech might be seen as radical, but it would be a great one. He would appeal to hope, imagination and opportunity. If anything could pull this off, it was his message that this was the chance of a lifetime. A controversial message and one which would require the party's support.

There was a knock at the door. "Mr Prime Minister?" a voice said. It was time. He rose to his feet, took a sip of water and looked in the mirror—yes, his tie was all right. Then, with decisive steps, he walked to the door.

INTRODUCTION

"And it ought to be remembered that there is nothing more difficult to take in hand, more perilous to conduct, or more uncertain in its success, than to take the lead in the introduction of a new order of things. Because the innovator has for enemies all those who have done well under the old conditions, and luke-warm defenders in those who may do well under the new."

NICCOLÒ MACHIAVELLI, IN 1505[1]

"We all know what to do, but we don't know how to get re-elected once we have done it."

JEAN-CLAUDE JUNCKER,
PRIME MINISTER OF LUXEMBOURG[2]

"All political lives end in failure because that is the nature of politics and of human affairs."

ENOCH POWELL, BRITISH CONSERVATIVE[3]

I HAVE BEEN TO PRAGUE, capital of the Czech Republic, three times—in 1993, 1999 and 2005. It is one of the most beautiful cities that I have visited. And so many things had visibly improved by my second visit, not to mention by the third. Houses were renovated, streets were cleaner, people had fashionable clothes, cars were newer, there were exclusive shops and service was better. The bartenders

---

[1] Machiavelli (2005).

[2] *The Economist* (2007c).

[3] *The Economist* (2007d).

suddenly knew how to make a mojito, and classical music poured out from several open windows. No more souvenirs from the Soviet Union on the street corners. Only the springtime sunshine and great beer seemed to be roughly the same as in the past.

This is progress in action—people's living standards rising. Society is changing, developing and improving. Not everything is great and there will always be new problems to solve. But many things have been improving for most people. In my view, and I think most people's too, this is very good and very important. For most of human history, absolute and desperate poverty has been the lot of almost everyone in the world. Wealth and progress have only come about during the last two centuries. Thus, it is actually wealth that is historically odd and has to be explained—poverty has been the rule. And wealth creation or progress in general cannot be taken for granted.

Isn't this stating the obvious? Not really. Progress has had many mighty enemies. Change as such creates counter-forces. Through history, strong religious and ideological forces have fought progress. And in today's society, many look back or see more risks than opportunities with the new. Having said this, however, politicians in the Western world have probably never before been so unanimously for growth as a leading aim for their policies as they are today. And the main conditions that lead to progress have probably never been as well established or accepted before. All political parties, except some extremists, support the main features of the market economy as the engine of progress and wealth creation.

This all leads to a mystery. Every country contains obstacles to change, progress and wealth creation. Reforms to improve the opportunities for a country and its citizens will always be important. And they are largely within the power of politicians to achieve. If most politicians want society to improve and know what the main conditions that lead there look like, why do they not do more to make it happen? Do they not want improvements? Or do they not know what should be done? Certainly, politicians do not actually create a wealthier society. But they set many conditions for those who unleash the forces of wealth creation—entrepreneurs, scientists, businessmen, investors and workers. There is no country in the world that cannot improve. So why do they not do it to a much greater extent?

This book is devoted to solving this alleged mystery. It is a book that stands for change, progress and wealth creation. Its purpose is to show that reform is important, possible to launch and that there are lessons about how to do it. By following a well-founded reform strategy, politicians can achieve political, economic and social gains. The first aim of the book is to inspire politicians to carry out more reform and show how they can do so—partly based on how others have done. It provides arguments for reform and explodes a number of myths. The second aim is to show economists and business people how politics works, and thereby how to successfully communicate with politicians. Society can improve much more than it does and a great number of problems today are completely unnecessary. Politicians may perceive that there are obstacles in the way, and indeed there are. But they can be overcome.

Wealth Creation

Why is there a need for reform—and what should reforms aim at? Wealthy countries have only existed for a fraction of human history. My own family is an illustration of how Sweden rapidly went from being a poor nation to becoming one of the wealthiest in Europe. My grandmother was born in a freezing cottage in the countryside, which is where most people lived in her day. Despite having abilities and interest, she had no opportunities to study. My father went to work in manufacturing industry, a tough job but with a substantially higher pay than my relatives working in agriculture had decades before. I have gone to university and work in the service sector, in a part of the knowledge economy.

Agriculture, industry and services: this is the route every country has taken from poverty to wealth. When a society develops and becomes more prosperous, people will have more opportunities to create the kind of life they desire. Today, the average income of a person in a West European country is about eight times higher in real terms than it was a century ago.[4] Studying the development of 16 industrialised countries since 1820, Angus Maddison has pointed out that their total economic output is 70 times higher today. Populations have increased strongly too, and average income per person is thus 14 times higher.[5] Wealth has been created, not redistributed from one person to another. This is also the development we can see now in large parts of Asia, though at a much faster rate.

In my view, this is the prime story of human achievement, and obstacles that are in the way of its continuation should be removed. Progress should not be delayed. One might object that it is more important that today's poor nations reach the living standards of the wealthy countries than it is for the wealthy to get even wealthier.[6] But they are not opposites; rather, they reinforce another. The speed of the rise of several poor countries today can be attributed to others having paved the way. They can go directly from no phones to mobile phones, without a century of landline phones in between.

---

[4] Baumol (2002).

[5] Maddison (1991).

And they need consumers in wealthy countries to be able to buy their new products.

Thus, the focus of my professional life has largely concerned identifying the conditions that make these continuous improvements possible. I think it is fairly uncontroversial to claim that the main conclusion is that progress demands change and change demands freedom, so many of my efforts are dedicated to advancing policies that increase freedom and thereby wealth creation. That is also the motivation for reform. Reform facilitates change, progress and wealth creation. I think most people agree that this aim is important, and one can always have a fruitful discussion about what the exact policies for achieving it might be. There is not just one way ahead but numerous ones. The bottom line is that it should be in everyone's prime interest to support reform.

Wealth first started growing as a consequence of trade links being forged as freedom increased when the Church and monarchies started to lose their grip. The Industrial Revolution really set Europe—as the first part of the world—on the path to prosperity. But the foundations were created earlier. The lack of central control in Europe due to its many fragmented nation-states, and their competition to shape the best laws and institutions, explains some of the first institutions of the free economy.[7] Today, we also see formerly poor countries motoring ahead, following policies that have opened up the economy. And the countries in the West that have the freest

---

[6] I deliberately use the terms "rich" or "wealthy" and "poor" when describing countries that are different in terms of GDP per capita rather than the terms "developed" and "developing", both because there are poor countries that are not developing and because I hope that today's wealthy countries will continue to develop.

[7] A fascinating account of these parts of Europe's economic history can be found in Rosenberg & Birdzell (1986).

economies have the highest prosperity, incomes and lowest unemployment.[8]

This does not mean that it is self-evident in every single case how the conditions for progress can improve. Neither is there any fixed type of society that would be perfect, nor only one model that can work. It is a complex world, and one may see the direction but not every single step forward. In the real world, countries have vastly different cultures, historic experiences and political systems. There is no utopia that should or could be pursued—change must be stepwise—but there are general principles. The state has fundamental tasks in society, but its scope also has to be restricted.

Progress is important and does not flow from nothing. DVD is better than VHS. A PC is better than a typewriter. The Internet is better than the telegraph. And that is just technological goods; many services have improved even more. The quality of transport, child care, hotels, health care, TV programmes and travel is of a rather different kind than a few decades ago. Every improvement starts with an idea that someone needs the freedom to develop. Entrepreneurs may need investors, import items, discuss with colleagues, protect their property, hire people, search for information and sell products. The fewer barriers for all such productive activities, the better.

A free society leads to a spontaneous development whose outcome cannot be predicted. It is impossible to know beforehand which ideas will come up tomorrow, let alone be successful. That is why there has to be freedom to experiment and fail.[9] Thus, we cannot know the nature of our work in the future. The majority of goods in today's world did

---

[8] Kane, Holmes & O'Grady (2007).

[9] Baumol (2002).

not exist in any form a century ago, and the future will be no different in that respect.[10] We can never know exactly what we will consume tomorrow. But history shows that the new will be better, or else people would not demand it. And we have to let the old goods, services, factories and jobs go. Otherwise the new will not arrive.

Joseph Schumpeter referred to this process as "creative destruction"—difficult, but necessary for progress.[11] The few per cent of the population in Western Europe who work in agriculture today produce more than the 70–90 per cent of the populations who were farmers in Western Europe did at the start of the 19th century.[12] Efficiency increased and most people went to do something else— largely work in manufacturing industry. Creative destruction may be difficult to explain, since the loss is concrete and the gain seems uncertain. Thus, there has always been a resistance to change. A telling symbol might be the rulers of Rostock in Germany in the 17th century, who ordered the murder of a spinning-machine inventor and the destruction of his work because they feared the invention would cause unemployment.

I am confident that my daughter Rebecka, soon two years old, will experience a constantly improving world. The main questions are how much better and how fast the development will be—and that is what we largely decide today when we carry out reforms or not. Ordinary people today live better than the medieval kings, not least in terms of life expectancy, health, knowledge and opportunities. And improvements have never been as rapid or dispersed to so many as they have during the last century and particularly the last few decades.

---

[10] Nordhaus (1997).

[11] Schumpeter (1975).

[12] Baumol (2002).

This will continue, and the fewer barriers, the quicker. Severe poverty is likely to be erased. Science will discover cures for serious diseases. We will be able to give more to our children than we could have imagined. What is luxury today will be everyday tomorrow.

Objections

Reforms should aim at facilitating progress and wealth creation. But there are objections to those aims. A common claim is that progress and increased growth is about "running faster" or "working more". But it is quite the opposite. For once, the pointy-haired boss in Dilbert was right when he said: "Work smarter, not harder." Wealth creation is about producing more value per hour worked. Innovators and competition drive this productivity growth. New technology, competence and organisation are methods for making this happen. And as we get more productive, we face the comfortable choice of continuing to work just as much and increasing our income, or settling for the same income and having more leisure time.

Nor does progress destroy the environment. Again, it is quite the opposite. In Europe, for example, the air, lakes and rivers are cleaner than they were a few decades ago, and the forests and secured natural areas are bigger.[13] This case has been thoroughly argued elsewhere.[14] When countries reach a certain level of wealth, their environmental impact tends to decrease.[15] Why do countries get greener as they get wealthier? Because the methods of production improve,

---

[13] OECD (2002a).

[14] See, for example, Goklany (2006); Lomborg (2001).

[15] The level is at roughly $10,000 annual GDP per capita, which has been passed by the wealthier parts of China already, and can be compared with the OECD average of $25,000.

consumers demand greener products, people can afford to look to the future and they want to leave a better world for their children. Now there are tendencies towards more environmentally friendly production in China, whose boom has so far partly damaged the environment.[16]

Another fashionable objection to prosperity is that it does not make people happier, and that happiness, after all, should be the most important aim in life. The leader of the UK Conservative party, David Cameron, has proposed adding a gross wellbeing product (GWP) measure to the traditional GDP measure.[17] It has been claimed that despite all the increases in wealth since 1945, we are not happier and that modern society makes us unhappier.[18] The most reliable and thorough research into wellbeing and happiness has shown, however, that we have never been as happy as we are today.[19] Furthermore, the happiest people live in the freest and richest countries— and nothing has created so much unhappiness as communism.[20] The Gallup World Poll, analysing 130 countries, has shown a strong correlation between a country's prosperity and its citizens' happiness.[21] The slow rise in happiness over the course of decades can be explained by rising expectations. If we suddenly had to live at 1945 standards, we would become rather unhappy.

Is there not a risk that many people will be left behind in this rapid development? That the strong will become highly affluent, leaving

---

[16] One analysis also interestingly showed that sulphur emissions are lower in those parts of China that have the greatest foreign trade, where foreign investments are large and competition strong. He (2007).

[17] Cameron (2006).

[18] Layard (2005).

[19] World Database of Happiness.

[20] Venhoven (1997).

[21] *The Economist* (2007h).

only scraps for the rest? One should bear in mind that wealth is the historically odd thing, so instead of everyone being poor, today only a minority is. And poverty will hardly decrease substantially in a society where incomes in general are not growing. In fact, remaining poverty—in rich and poor countries alike—can largely be explained with limits on people's freedom to create a better life. The lack of property rights, for example, prevents many poor farmers from getting a loan that they could invest in their farm to increase productivity or start a new business.[22] Such limits to opportunity can explain much of the poverty in rich countries too, for instance labour market entry barriers that keep many young people and immigrants out.

Still, change can be hard and people get different starting points in life. A central feature of a good society, in my view, must be real opportunities for everyone. As a child, I had many talented friends who did not go to university just because they did not have that tradition at home or were even discouraged by their family. It is a pity and a waste. How our lives end up, all other things being equal, should be decided by our individual capabilities, not those of our parents. Social mobility is a crucial feature of a fair society. Those—often on the political right—who do not care or simply call this a free choice are ignorant. And those on the left who think everyone should earn roughly the same regardless of education or effort take away the increased income as an incentive for those without a tradition to study.

Obstacles to Wealth Creation

Reforms should remove obstacles to progress. But where did the obstacles come from? Of course, there will never be an ideal society

---

[22] De Soto (2000).

and conditions can always improve. This is something the state can do, for example by laws that protect property. But state interventions have largely had quite the opposite aims and effects. Many obstacles are remnants from an old, authoritarian society and several of them are newer. After World War II, many countries chose to expand the size of the state as a share of society.[23] The centrally planned war economy was perceived as superior to the market economy and the visible hand was widely considered better than the invisible one.[24] Taxes increased radically, companies were nationalised, markets were regulated, welfare services delivered by public monopolies and social security systems, such as pensions, run by the state.

This was partly an ideological matter. But parties change and during this period most parties—at least in Europe—were united behind the aim of expanding the state.[25] They simply believed that a centrally planned system was more efficient and fair. And they said they would improve lives for ordinary people as a matter of social justice. Research has since produced substantial evidence to suggest that the self-interest of bureaucracy in growth was a major driving force behind the expansion.[26] It was also in the self-interest of politicians of all political parties to make promises paid for by taxpayers in order to win elections, including favours to special interests.[27]

The market economy was considered old-fashioned, unstable and unfair. A modern society should plan its future and decide about it

---

[23] In this book, I have chosen to refer to the size of the state—as a share of society as a whole—and not the size of Government, which is quite commonly used in the public debate. The term Government here refers only to the executive branch of the decision-making system in a country.

[24] The debate of that time is thoroughly described in Blundell (2005).

[25] In the case of Sweden, this case has been shown in Uddhammar (1993).

[26] See Buchanan (2000–).

[27] Olson (1982).

democratically; the majority was considered to be right. According to John Maynard Keynes, the state at the very least should affect the business cycle by borrowing in bad times and saving in good times.[28] It should play the main role in creating wealth and building a new society, from housing to child care and pensions. After World War II, many economists believed that there would be a stepwise merger between the centrally planned economies and the formerly free-market ones—in some kind of mixed economic system.[29] In those days, few politicians saw a limit to how much the state could and should do in society. Everything was just about expansion.

I described this development in my last main book, "European Dawn", and somewhat provocatively claimed that this created more problems than it solved.[30] The expanded role of the state produced many results that were not very social. Many aims might have been decent, but the method was based on false assumptions. The state can never centrally plan the future, a monopoly is not efficient, and innovators need freedom. A few, like Friedrich Hayek, realised this at an early stage.[31] But for most, the collapse of the Soviet Union was probably the ultimate proof. So the development of an ever larger state stopped and went into reverse. Starting in the UK, the market economy underwent a renaissance. New Labour today is more market-oriented that most centre-right parties were in Europe in the 1970s.

---

[28] His main arguments for that case can be found in Keynes (1936).

[29] See, for example, Dillard (1967).

[30] Munkhammar (2005).

[31] Hayek (1944).

A Need for Reform

The growth of the state stopped and was even reversed in some areas of society. We have seen macroeconomic stabilisation and new institutions, deregulated product markets and monetary and tax reforms. The results are very clear. Extremely controversial as the shift was at the time, the evidence of improvements is undeniable. A person visiting not only Prague but Tallinn or Bratislava today compared to a decade or two ago will see the difference everywhere. Indeed, that also goes for London, Dublin and Stockholm. People are healthier, live longer, eat better, have higher incomes, enjoy a cleaner environment and are happier and more optimistic than they were a few decades ago. It is also relevant to note that the reforms in question have been pursued by governments labelled as left or right alike.[32]

The fact that the state stopped growing when it had reached a very impressive size was not by definition a free-market revolution. It has been said that "Socialism is dead, but Leviathan lives". The idea of the state running almost everything probably appeals to relatively few people today, but the kind of society which emerged from such a vision is largely still in place. Yes, the market economy had a renaissance in several ways, but to a very different degree in different countries. Some nations went ahead with fairly bold reforms. But many others did not, and here many obstacles to progress and wealth creation remain. The evidence for what should be done is massive and the success stories apparent: even those countries that have carried out limited reforms have often had surprisingly positive results. Yet little is happening.

---

[32] See, for example, Williamson & Haggard (1994). The book will provide more examples from OECD countries.

Society has really changed since the 1950s, not to mention that it is changing right now and the speed of that process is continuously increasing:

* Globalisation has created new markets, empowered new consumers and increased specialisation. More people than ever are part of the global workforce, but another billion are on their way in. The world economy is booming, the new quickly replaces the old and competition is often fierce.[33]

* Structural change in the business sector is getting faster. The shift away from employment in manufacturing industry to service production, a sector that already employs roughly seven out of ten people in the EU, continues. This raises questions about productivity, welfare services, trade and the taxation of work.[34]

* Our societies are becoming more heterogeneous. We study abroad, watch foreign TV and have different religions and attend different schools, while companies have international owners. State provision of collective solutions for everyone becomes less legitimate, and heterogeneous societies normally have more limited government.[35]

* The average citizen is getting older, which is a great success but increases demand for several welfare services that are currently tax-financed. And the state today provides strong incentives to retire at a certain, rather low, age. A substantial need exists for reform.[36]

---

[33] Many fascinating stories about the new opportunities created in today's world can be studied in Friedman (2005).

[34] The case of lower productivity growth in the services sector is developed in Baumol (1967).

[35] Alesina & Glaeser (2004).

[36] The need for reforms of demographic reasons in a number of countries is described in Jackson & Howe (2003), an index which also makes an assessment of how serious the need is in different countries is.

Economics and Politics

Economists often look at politicians with a good deal of contempt. They simply do not see how it can be rational for a politician not to carry out the reforms that are certain to have such good effects, so they think politicians are irrational. Economists usually refer to the unpredictable element of politicians' behaviour as "political reasons". I have worked closely with prominent businessmen with a great talent for leading multinational companies who cannot understand why politicians do not do the right thing. A fundamental part of understanding obstacles to reform—and seeing the way past them—is to take a politician's perspective. Politicians are as rational as anyone— from their perspective. To most people, that is a new world. But it is the world of those with the power to make changes that can improve the situation for the rest of us immensely. Economic analysis often takes off in the marketplace, but the political arena is fundamentally different.

I used to be a member of the Swedish Liberal party (liberal in the European sense) and was a member of the board of the national youth organisation and a candidate for both the national and European parliaments. It is striking to see the course of debate in a political party in terms of policies and proposals. I once participated in a discussion with several MPs about the party platform for the upcoming election. The question was whether the party should propose an increase in sales tax to be able to propose a decrease in labour taxes? And the discussion started. Did anyone talk about tax bases? Effects on consumption? Or effects on employment? Nobody talked about the issue at all. The main point, made by one MP and indicative of the whole discussion, was: "How would I ever be able to explain that proposal to people outside the supermarket when I hold election campaign meetings?"

Economists and businessmen might say that this confirms their image of politicians. Fairly often their proposal is: "Educate them!" This is neither feasible nor desirable, and most importantly it is beside the point. Just like everyone else, politicians may not know everything, but that is not the main reason for their action or inaction. Politics is a totally different arena and rationality than economics and business. Political considerations like those mentioned are perfectly natural parts of a democratic system. What really matters is to get to know the true nature of the incentives for politicians. Research into this has many names, such as political economy, political science, political equilibrium and public choice. Great effort has gone into examining the obstacles, but not enough into how to get the incentives right. How can politicians feel that they will be rewarded if they actually press for change and pursue reforms in everyone's interest?

Politicians know that they have to get elected to have any influence at all. And when they are elected, they have to keep a strong position in order to be a force for change. At times, when I have communicated a radical message on the need for substantial change, I have received similar reactions from leading politicians. "We know, you're perfectly right, but we can't say that," they say. It may be a little frustrating, but I do know that they cannot just say it. There are too many traditions, stakeholders, vested interests, relationships, conflicts and opponents. That is what a modern, democratic society is like; it is pluralistic and dynamic. Not only is it hard to know what in a single case provides the greatest benefit to society as a whole—it is also difficult to pursue. And elections do not always benefit reformers. However, none of this means that substantial change is possible or that it takes a political superman to reform a country.

I felt very strongly the limits to how difficult it is to set the agenda of the public debate when I had a key role in one of the largest political campaigns in Swedish history, the "Yes to the Euro" campaign before the 2003 referendum. By the way, yes, I am in favour of the single market and the euro, but against harmful interventions by the EU such as subsidies, labour market regulations and tax harmonisation. The euro campaign had hired most every policy and communications expert in and outside the country. But when we had planned a day of a hundred activities about the euro and trade, suddenly the news was all about Germany not meeting the demands of the Stability and Growth Pact. Despite having extensive resources, our abilities were limited. And in the end, a clear majority voted no. Politicians sometimes say that this is what they feel all the time. Ninety per cent of a day is crisis management, nine per cent is reacting to what others do and one per cent is something proactive. This is natural in a pluralistic, open, society, but it is also a factor in the prospects for achieving reform. The schedule is tight and it usually takes real effort to gain some control.

Politics is a complex art of strategy, alliance-building, communication, loyalty, conflicts, historic relations and tactics. The political landscape, which partly decides what is possible and not in terms of reform, is a minefield. Every country needs reforms, though to different degrees, and every country has reformers—and the degree of obstacles they face differs too. Politics is the art of the possible, and not everything is possible. You cannot just identify a problem, find a solution and then do it. If change is to last, it has to be done cleverly, and a long-term strategy can expand the sphere of what is possible. Of course, there must be incentives to do the right thing. But contrary to what politicians sometimes believe, they do not just have to sit and wait for the right moment to turn up or the landscape to change. The ways to implement a successful change might already be there, but they might be unaware of it. One of the primary aims of this book is to describe "how", in order to inspire politicians to do and dare more.

I talked to a former deputy minister of finance who said that for many years during the 1980s, the finance ministry had stored many reform proposals on the shelf, ready to launch. Only the launches did not happen—due to heavy resistance from most directions—until a severe economic crisis hit the country. Then, most of the proposals were launched within weeks and accepted by everyone a few years after implementation. People often think it takes a crisis to make substantial reforms possible, but in fact countries have completed major reforms without being in total crisis. The former deputy minister said the window of reform opportunity suddenly opened up and then there were politicians ready to use it. The important question is what actually opens that window, and then, what kind of leadership it takes to launch reforms successfully. And, of course, that there are proposals which are ready to launch.

If politicians perceive that it is not in their interest to carry out reform they will make great efforts to avoid it. They may give numerous reasons for inaction, such as saying that people are against reforms, that the proposals will not work, that change is unnecessary, that some group will suffer, that special interests will protest, and so on. During a positive business cycle, as in recent years, they may claim that the good times demonstrate that reforms are not necessary. A common mistake is to believe that the reasons which politicians use to argue a certain standpoint are their real reasons for the standpoint. This is usually not the case. They communicate with arguments they believe can convince others. But what once convinced them might be something totally different.[37] What matters is to find out what actually convinces politicians to undertake reform. And when that happens, there will be action and the politicians will use all sorts of arguments to convince others.

---

[37] There are analyses on this topic for example in Bardach (2005).

The Crossroads

There are more than two main paths—reform or not reform—to the future. The political response to problems can turn into something that makes those problems even worse: namely, counter-reform. Again, politicians may not believe that the measures would have positive effects but they believe they might gain politically from carrying them out. For decades, Argentina was an example of this, with the protectionist Péronists returning to power several times and always doing the wrong things and making the situation worse.[38] The problems may be blamed on immigrants, globalisation, companies or "evil forces" in general. And the measures following such a deeply flawed description of reality will be counterproductive and thus make the problems even worse. Society gets thrown into a negative spiral of inwardness, hostility, unemployment, crime and poverty.[39]

Anyone looking at the public debate during the past years will see tendencies in quite a few directions. Some political voices have argued for tax cuts, trade in services, openness to immigration, deregulated labour markets, private competition in health care—in other words, openness and reform. Equally, some voices have talked about "economic patriotism", no more Polish plumbers, no trade in services, blocks on international corporate mergers, subsidies to "national champions" and shutting out the rest of the world. This is a classic battle. And this is the crossroads at which the OECD stands: change or trying to stop change. Of course, not all countries will take the same measures and no country is likely to walk exclusively down one of these paths. But the more reform, and the less reactionary

---

[38] Rojas (2003).

[39] The mechanisms of that negative spiral are outlined in Kreuger (1974).

protectionism, the better. Finding ways for politicians to do the right thing is therefore of the utmost importance for the future.

A Guide

Many questions need to be answered: What does the case for reform look like? Why is there a need for reform? Where are reforms needed? How differently do countries perform? How much can countries actually learn from others? What have the main results from reforms been? Where do ideas for reform policies actually come from? How do they get onto the political agenda? Does it take a severe economic crisis to trigger reform? Is it easier for small countries to reform? Should reforms be done stepwise or all at once (a so-called big bang)? How important is popular support and how should popular protests be handled? Does it matter what parts of society initiate reform and, if so, where should one start? How should special interests be handled? What are the necessary elements of a successful communications strategy for reform? Do differences exist between systems of checks and balances and parliamentary systems? When is an appropriate time to launch reforms? What are the roles of international organisations, the media and think-tanks?

This is a guide to reform. Like all guidebooks, it aims to show the easiest way to the best sites. All OECD countries will be visited, with longer stays in countries that have reformed substantially. What did they do and how did they do it? Along the way, there will be a stop or two in countries that tried but failed. There will also some travelling in the fields of theory and research. A look at some models and experiments reveals a lot. What are the main conclusions on obstacles to reform and the methods to get past them? Naturally, there will be some trips into history and examinations of society of today. Why is there a need for reform and what kind of reforms are needed—and where? Last but not least, there will be stops to look at the situation of politicians. How do they perceive reality and what is the rationality on which politicians base their actions?

Summary and Conclusions

Progress and wealth creation are vital to society. They demand change, and change has always had many enemies. Reform is about tearing down barriers to change and progress. Every country needs reform, but the degree differs. Countries that have reformed have often rapidly become more prosperous. This has not only increased incomes, but also led to environmental improvements and increased happiness. Social indicators have improved. Reforms is largely about decreasing state intervention in society. Several fundamental trends in society, such as globalisation and demographics, create a strong need for reform in today's wealthy countries. Yet very little is happening in most nations. This can be explained by a number of mechanisms in the political arena. But countries can reform; the political incentives just have to be there. This book will show the different types of reform implemented in different countries, explore the need for reform, identify obstacles and show how to do it.

ONE SIZE FITS ALL?

"Can the Ethiopian change his skin, or the leopard his spots?"

THE BIBLE, JEREMIAH

"We demand guaranteed rigidly defined areas of doubt and uncertainty."

DOUGLAS ADAMS

"There are known knowns. These are things we know that we know. There are known unknowns. That is to say, there are things that we know we don't know. But there are also unknown unknowns. There are things we don't know we don't know."

DONALD RUMSFELD,
FORMER UNITED STATES SECRETARY OF DEFENCE

ALL COUNTRIES ARE DIFFERENT IN numerous ways: geographic, cultural, religious, economic, political, constitutional and historic, to name a few. To what extent can countries actually be compared—and how much can they learn from one another? Every country can improve by getting rid of unnecessary obstacles to progress and wealth creation. But to what extent do countries actually have similar problems—or relevant solutions? What if most problems are unique for every country, stemming from country-specific origins? Can politicians affect the fate of the country, or is it mainly decided by factors out of reach? If the latter is true, the case for reform is weak.

Take a few examples. High employment is sometimes explained by, say, "the Lutheran work ethic" rather than policies. But even though that may be part of the explanation, it cannot be a major part, since there are Protestant countries with low employment and Catholic countries with high employment. Estonia's great success sometimes is attributed to it being such a small country. If that were a decisive factor, why would Haiti be one of the world's poorest countries? And why would some of China's success simultaneously be attributed to its vast size and labour supply? It is sometimes claimed that a severe crisis is necessary as a trigger for reform. Again, this might sometimes be a factor but it does not explain the continuous reforms in places like Australia, Spain, the Netherlands and Iceland. Some claim that reform has only occurred in English-speaking countries, but surely reformist nations like Estonia, Spain, Slovakia, Sweden and Iceland are not part of that group?[40]

Countries are very different in terms of size, position and natural resources. Montesquieu famously wrote that climate substantially influences society, making the point that colder countries simply have to go to more effort to create a good society.[41] And the geographical size of a country might have an impact, a factor that has usually been determined by numerous historical factors. One study argued that a large country can experience more economies of scale but may find it more difficult to formulate policies, since the population tends to be more heterogeneous.[42] There are also many historical examples showing that countries with access to the sea have found it easier to initiate trade and hence foster economic growth.[43] The existence of

---

[40] In a report, former OECD Chief Economist David Henderson elaborates somewhat on this issue: Henderson (1996).

[41] Montesquieu (1748).

[42] Alesina & Spolaore (2003).

[43] Norberg (2003).

natural resources, or not, may be relevant to a country's economic prospects.

These are a few fundamental differences. How important are they in explaining countries' economic development? Of course, they can be important but they cannot be of a decisive character. For example, there are also small countries that are heterogeneous and therefore may find it harder to formulate policies. There are countries close to the sea that still have not experienced a boost in trade or economic growth, especially in Africa. And there are countries without access to the sea that have built great prosperity, like Switzerland. Furthermore, there are countries with vast natural resources that have not done particularly well yet (parts of Asia, for example) and very successful countries with practically no natural resources (like Hong Kong or Japan). One telling example of the role of natural resources is water. In some of the most naturally water-rich countries in the world, people do not have access to clean water, but people do in some of the world's driest countries.[44]

How important, then, is religion for economic development? Quite a lot has been written about this. Max Weber argued that the Protestant Reformation was critical to the rise of capitalism.[45] One reason might be that people then knew little of each other, though if many were members of the same church it provided some common ground for trust and thus business relations. Some have found evidence that the more religious—in particular Christian—beliefs there are in a society, the higher the per-capita GDP. However, it has also been pointed out that in very religious societies there is sometimes a tendency to disregard the work of women, which is negative to

---

[44] Segerfeldt (2005).

[45] Weber (2002).

43

growth.[46] Another study disputed the correlation between Christianity and growth, partly by making comparisons of different religious groups within countries, finding that Islam is no less positively correlated to growth.[47] It is also a well established conclusion that the historic partial retreat of the Catholic Church to the spiritual world, whereby it ceased to prohibit a number of free economic activities, was important for the rise of capitalism.[48]

The latter point leads to a relevant conclusion—which might in several countries be within politicians' reach—about the need to separate government and religion. Progress and wealth creation did indeed start off in Europe but this was mainly a consequence of factors other than Christian religion. It had more to do with the fragmentation of the European nations, and the lack of central control, which made possible an institutional competition towards stepwise improvements of policies and institutions.[49] Today, wealth is being created not only in countries where people mainly believe in Christianity, but also in nations like India and China which are dominated by Hinduism and Buddhism. Religion has had a role, but it is not the main explanation for progress.

Another fundamental difference between countries is the political system. The first and major difference is between dictatorships and democracies. According to Freedom House, which performs an annual assessment of the degree of political freedom in countries around the world, there were 90 "free" countries in 2006, representing 47 per cent of the world's population. In 1976, there were only 42 free

---

[46] Guiso, Sapienza & Zingales (2002).

[47] Noland (2003).

[48] Rosenberg & Birdzell (1986).

[49] Landes (1998).

countries, representing a mere 26 per cent of the world's population. We have seen a wave of democratisation, mainly in the 1990s, though Freedom House concludes that this been slower over the last ten years. Indeed, political freedom has even declined in parts of Asia, mainly in Russia. The number of "partly free" countries in 2006 was 58 and the number of "not free" was 45.[50]

In a dictatorship, political power is centralised and people's political freedoms are severely restricted. There may sometimes be similar needs for economic reform in dictatorships and democracies, not least because a dictatorship often puts barriers in the way of wealth creation. It is hardly a coincidence that the poorest countries are also dictatorships. Political tyranny does not make free-market reforms more likely. Wealth creation in the long run demands openness, which undermines tyranny; a wealthy middle class is ultimately likely to demand more political freedom; and an advanced economy needs a society of free thought to be at the cutting edge of innovation and research. In any case, every aspect of a political reform strategy differs between dictatorships and democracies. This book focuses on democracies.

Differences exist between the design of the political institutions and systems in democracies too.[51] A major initial difference is between parliamentary democracies and those based on checks and balances. In a parliamentary system, the government is usually formed by the majority in parliament, so the government and majority are the same. In a system of checks and balances, the executive and legislative branches are more separated and also elected separately. There might therefore be separate political majorities in such a system,

---

[50] Freedom House (2007).

[51] See, for example, Cheibub (2006).

which has often been the case in the US and France. In a system of checks and balances, the "political efficiency" might be lower, meaning it may be harder to launch new policies. There is evidence that the state is smaller as a share of society in presidential regimes.[52] A major division within parliamentary democracies is between those with proportional representation and those with first-past-the-post electoral systems. It is easier to get a strong majority government in first-past-the-post systems than in proportional ones. This will determine the government's degree of power and ease of action.

A further major difference between countries is whether they are centralised states or federations with a substantial independence of member states or regions. France and Sweden are highly centralised, whereas Germany and especially Switzerland are more decentralised. In a federal system, the public sphere at federal (national) level is more limited and regions or member states have a substantial degree of political sovereignty. This can have two main effects. First, it is harder for the federal government to implement nationwide policies. Second, there will be more institutional competition between regions, which promotes economic growth.[53]

Numerous differences exist between national political systems. In the real world, every country is unique. Does this imply that one nation can learn nothing or very little from another? Are the needs for reform, obstacles to reform and strategies to reform by definition totally different? No, it just means that there are limits to comparisons and that national political systems cannot be too different for similar conclusions to be made or reform strategies to be applicable. Hence, a choice has to be made regarding which countries to study

---

[52] Persson & Tabellini (1998).

[53] Feld, Zimmerman & Döring (2004).

and which countries to learn from and to direct reform advice to. This book is thus only focused on lessons from democracies to other democracies. Despite the substantial divisions even within that group, the political terrain in which politicians and policymakers move is fundamentally the same for democracies. There are voters, the media, an opposition and NGOs—to mention a few common and relevant factors.

One last major difference between countries is their degree of prosperity. Naturally, wealthy countries and poor countries do not need the same kinds of reform. They are on different levels of development, with different structures of production and indeed different obstacles to reform. In poor countries, heavy bureaucracy—three times the administrative costs compared to wealthy countries on average—and weak property rights are two main obstacles to people doing business. 40 per cent of the economy in poor countries is, on average, informal.[54] Many poor countries need to build effective institutions, provide basic property rights to their populations, open up for trade and fight severe corruption.[55]

Most wealthy countries do not face those sorts of challenge today. This is not to say that the experience from today's wealthy countries is irrelevant for the poorer ones. On the contrary, emulating successful features of the wealthier societies is one way to success. The countries of Africa, Asia and South America that largely followed the socialist or protectionist path have had the worst development, just like the countries in Europe that ended up in such systems. And the (mainly Asian) countries that have liberalised their economies the

---

[54] The World Bank, Doing Business 2005, Removing Obstacles to Growth, World Bank, International Finance Corporation, Oxford University Press, 2005, http://www.doingbusiness.org

[55] The World Bank (2007b).

most have enjoyed lasting success. It started with Japan in the 1960s. Singapore and Hong Kong followed, and now China and India are booming. In economic terms, they are characterised mainly by low taxes, an export orientation, small public social transfers, a conservative macroeconomic policy, strong education and free labour markets.[56]

Similar economic and political institutions have created successful societies wherever they have been introduced. This does not imply that there should be no variations between taxes, social systems, trade regulations or labour markets in the world. On the contrary, policy innovations will always differ when countries compete to find the best solutions. This is a race that never ends since institutions will never be perfect and society is ever-changing. For reform proposals to be relevant, the economic starting-point of the countries advised must be roughly similar. Also, the obstacles to reform faced by policymakers in wealthy countries are different from those in poor countries, so the strategies to get past them must be too. This book will therefore focus on today's wealthy democracies, which in practice are the OECD member states.

Numerous differences also exist between the OECD countries and these might explain some variations in policies and degree of reform. Economic performance in Germany, Italy and France has been poorer than in the United States, Britain and Canada. This is also correlated with a number of differing values among citizens in those countries. The latter three countries generally have substantially higher shares of the citizens that want a job offering opportunities for achievement, chances for initiative, and want to take responsibility and have freedom. It is difficult to know whether those values evolved from policies

---

[56] Åslund (2007b).

48

or vice versa. Perhaps values change as policies change? Professor Edmund S Phelps writes that he "…had not imagined that Continental Man might be less entrepreneurial" and points to possible historical explanations.[57] Which values people have in a society will affect its development, but values change with development too—and policies might lead to new values.

Clearly, history matters. All countries have their own histories, though of course, these have evolved in relation with other countries. No country can be taken out of historical context when analysing why reforms do or do not take place. There is always a degree of "path dependence", where—for different reasons—countries may stick to old systems, models or policies. Society develops incrementally, building on previous steps. A number of forces always work to preserve the old.[58] This does not mean that a country's history will dictate its future or that change is impossible. But historic facts may make the same reform more difficult in one country than in another. Change in general also demands some effort and has to build on the past. Such factors have to be taken into account when analysing reforms in OECD countries, as well as attempting to emulate the solutions and applying similar reform strategies. Solutions may be similar, but there are always local conditions to adapt them to.

Summary and Conclusions

Every country is unique, made unique by numerous factors throughout the path of history. Countries are different in size, geography,

---

[57] Phelps (2007a).

[58] Paul A David makes a very strong case for this view in David (2000). However, I believe that his conclusion about the degree of difficulty in changing the development of a country goes too far.

culture, religion and values. In many ways, these factors are also interrelated. History does not determine the future of a country, but it matters. Most of these factors are not within reach of politicians to change, and attempts to do it are probably not desirable. However, the decisive factors determining whether a country has become wealthy or not are none of these. Countries that have adopted certain economic and political institutions have been able to become wealthy. Countries differ in terms of political system and economic level too. Though there are differences among democracies, the main difference is between dictatorships and democracies. Thus, this book only analyses democracies, since they offer relevant lessons for other democracies. Poor countries are in need of reform, but not the same reforms as their rich counterparts. This book therefore focuses on lessons from and to OECD countries.

A CHANGING WORLD

"Weep not that the world changes—did it keep a stable, changeless state, it were cause indeed to weep."

WILLIAM CULLEN BRYANT

"Only three things in life are certain: birth, death and change."

ARABIC PROVERB

PROGRESS DEMANDS CHANGE. NEW IDEAS lead to innovations and products that are superior to the old ones. Numerous changes have taken place as society has developed. Old products give way for new ones, old ways of organising are replaced by new ones, old jobs disappear and new ones are created. The need to reform is rooted largely in the fact that public institutions, systems, laws or regulations have become obsolete or harmful in societies that are different from a few decades earlier, perhaps putting barriers in the way of change and progress. The number of separate changes is incalculable but they can be described as a few main trends that point in a certain direction. Increasing globalisation, demographics and technological factors constitute three long-term trends that contribute more for every passing day to the need for reform.

Globalisation

Globalisation is a popular term used to describe a number of trends, changes and developments in the world today. There are economic, political, cultural and environmental aspects. Barriers to economic exchange and mobility for information, capital, goods and services are fewer, which means there is more trade and investment across national borders than ever before. The world has experienced periods of globalisation before, not least before World War I, but the scale is of a different dimension today. Many global issues have become local, and we are much more interdependent. Prices of many goods are falling, benefiting consumers. The share of the world's population that has an income of only $1 per day or less fell from 40.4 per cent in 1981 to 18.4 per cent in 2004 or, expressed in absolute numbers, from 1,482 million to 985 million.[59] There are telling differences within that group: poor countries that were open to globalisation grew on average by 5 per cent annually during the 1990s. Those that were protectionist saw their economies shrink by an annual average of 1 per cent.[60]

Globalisation enhances the need for reform. First of all, countries that are more open to globalisation—trade and investments—are wealthier. Reforms to open up a country to the world and avoid protectionism are thus important. Second, the pace of change generally increases. Because there are more people, ideas, innovators and consumers in the world, improvements in goods and services are faster. Old goods, services and jobs have to go. Attempts to protect the old not only stop the new but only temporarily delay the inevitable loss of the old. Third, globalisation increases competition for investments,

---

[59] The World Bank (2007a).
[60] Collier & Dollar (2002).

production and, ultimately, jobs. In one way, countries do not compete—companies do. One of a national government's main tasks is to give domestic companies very good conditions in which to compete.

The OECD has measured the degree of outward-looking policies in its member countries, for example concerning trade and investments. In every country except one, policies became more outward-looking between 1998 and 2003.[61] Thomas Friedman has pointed out that this era of globalisation really started with the fall of the Berlin Wall and that we are now in Globalisation 3.0, which levels out the world and makes it easier for hundreds of millions of people in poor countries to compete. One point about the current level of globalisation is that very much lower transaction and co-ordination costs mean that competition is no longer really between firms but between people within firms who are performing similar tasks in different countries.[62] When people with similar levels of productivity in another country can perform the same things at a fraction of the price, there is an incentive to offshore parts of the production. Anyone trying to continue producing the same things in such a situation will see wages fall, which underlines the need to have a dynamic, flexible and creative society where new production emerges.

One way to illustrate the new world is to show the strength of growth in many emerging economies. Figure 1 shows the share of global output produced by fast-growing Asian nations. In a study, PricewaterhouseCoopers has compared the G7—today's wealthiest countries—with the E7—the emerging economies. They point out that the economy of G7 is today 25 per cent larger than that of the E7, and estimate that in 2050, E7 will be 75 per cent larger than G7.

---

[61] Conway & Nicoletti (2005).

[62] Baldwin (2006).

53

FIGURE 1. DEVELOPING ASIA'S* SHARE OF GLOBAL OUTPUT, 1980–2006.

Developing Asia's GDP (PPP) as a percentage of World GDP (PPP)

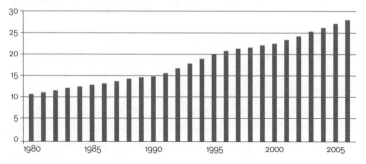

*Developing Asia: Bangladesh, Bhutan, Cambodia, China, Fiji, India, Indonesia, Kiribati, Lao People's Democratic Republic, Malaysia, Maldives, Myanmar, Nepal, Pakistan, Papua New Guinea, Philippines, Samoa, Solomon Islands, Sri Lanka, Thailand, Tonga, Vanuatu, Vietnam.

Source: IMF World Economic Outlook Database

Average income per person in the world will be 50 per cent higher in 2020 compared to 2000, according to the US National Intelligence Council. The council also argues that the benefits of an increased globalisation will accrue most to countries that can access and adopt new technologies.[63] Conclusions include strong advice for today's rich nations to avoid protectionism, subsidies and traditional industrial policy.[64] Which countries, then, are the most globalised?

A T Kearney Inc and the Carnegie Endowment for International Peace conduct an annual assessment of the degree of globalisation in 62 countries which account for 96 per cent of the world's economic output and 85 per cent of the population. The survey looks at personal, economic, political and technological indicators. Above are the

---

[63] National Intelligence Council (2004).
[64] Hawksworth (2006).

27 OECD countries that are part of the Index, in descending order. Number one in the complete list is Singapore, which is not an OECD member. One conclusion in the 2006 edition of the Index is that countries have become more globalised during the last years.

TABLE 1. DEGREE OF GLOBALISATION, OECD COUNTRIES, 2006[65]

1. Switzerland	15. Germany
2. United States	16. Hungary
3. Ireland	17. France
4. Denmark	18. Portugal
5. Canada	19. Spain
6. Netherlands	20. Slovak Republic
7. Australia	21. Italy
8. Austria	22. Japan
9. Sweden	23. Korea
10. New Zealand	24. Greece
11. United Kingdom	25. Poland
12. Finland	26. Mexico
13. Norway	27. Turkey
14. Czech Republic	

Source: A T Kearney Inc and the Carnegie Endowment for International Peace

Advice about how to be attractive, competitive and successful in a more globalised world first of all emphasises openness. The gains from foreign trade are as well-founded in economic theory as they are vast. One study described the gains for the United States: "We find that trade opening since World War II has added between $800

[65] Kearney (2006). Belgium, Iceland and Luxembourg are not among the 62 on the 2006 list, for unknown reasons, which is why there are only 27 and not 30 OECD countries on the list.

billion to $1.4 trillion to the US economy, or about $7,000 to $13,000 per household. More speculative estimates of the potential additional gains from removing the rest of US trade barriers range from $400 billion to $1.3 trillion, or about $4,000 to $12,000 per household. Since trade opening permanently raises national income, these gains are enjoyed annually."[66]

A country should create good conditions for investment, work and education—that is, productive activities. And flexibility is important in terms of being able to let the old go and allow for the new to emerge. Policy implications of this have to do with lower and simpler taxes, freer markets and fewer regulations for entrepreneurs. Countries that have been more open to globalisation have found it easier to fund various social and welfare programmes, since openness makes business more competitive.[67] This shows that not only does the size and scope of the public sphere matter, it also matters what the public sphere is doing. Where the state has a role, it should facilitate change, not delay it. Areas where this may be relevant include a more flexible education system and retraining, as well as policies to get unemployed back to work.

What about migration? One element of globalisation is the mobility of people, which has not increased in the way that mobility for goods, investments and to some degree services has. Though there are still millions of refugees in the world, moving involuntarily, people face many restrictions on their ability to voluntarily and legally move to OECD countries. In the US, there has been a long debate about illegal immigration and in Europe, the latest enlargements of the EU have created new barriers to mobility. Doubtlessly, migration stirs up

---

[66] Summary of Bradford, Grieco, & Hufbauer (2006).

[67] Bergh (2006).

emotions, but there are many arguments for reforms that free up mobility.

People would not move if they did not benefit personally. But there are also a number of benefits for the countries they move to. Many immigrants tend to become entrepreneurs, which benefits society by creating jobs and growth. Considering the demographics in many countries, there is definitely a demand for more people of working age, though it has to be remembered that the immigrants will eventually get older too. There are also arguments about open and diverse countries being more dynamic and creative. Some fear a "brain drain" in the countries that people leave, but that seems largely unfounded. The migrants often return again, with more skills—and their remittances to people at home while away far exceed the state foreign aid programmes to the same countries.[68] Adverse effects of migration are largely created by harmful policies and cannot be ignored. They should lead to policy changes to make integration work.

Another long-term trend, partly connected to globalisation, is the increasing heterogeneity of Western society. In other words, the citizens of France, Germany, Sweden and Ireland have less and less in common with their fellow countrymen. Some countries have always been rather diverse, but this has been increasing for most countries. Half a century ago, people in the same country may have watched roughly the same TV programmes, read the same daily papers, attended similar schools and were members of the same church. They had stayed in the same jobs for decades, were born in the country and had done military service. All in all, therefore, they shared more similar values and views. Today, this is less the case. We study

---

[68] A thorough account of many arguments for immigration can be found in Legrain (2007).

abroad, travel to distant parts of the world, change jobs, get information via the internet and many of us are immigrants. A German doctor may feel that he has more in common with a Danish doctor than he has with a German IT engineer. This has potential implications for the need and demand for reform. There is evidence that people do not consider collective government solutions or redistribution legitimate when people have less in common.[69]

Demography

We live longer than ever before, which must surely be considered one of humanity's great achievements. This, combined with the fact that many countries have rather low birth rates, means that populations are ageing. In some OECD countries, such as Germany, populations are actually falling, in stark contrast to the fear a few decades ago of global overpopulation. In Europe, the decrease is particularly noticeable in its Eastern and Central parts. In 1950, 20 per cent of the world's population lived in Europe. In 2005, the share was 11 per cent and in 2050 it is forecast to be 7 per cent.[70] This not only reflects the decrease in Europe, but also that other parts of the world will have growing populations. In the OECD, the US will also continue to grow but Japan will have a substantially decreasing population. Demographic forecasts for the long-term perspective are fairly certain, since everyone who will potentially retire in 2050 has already been born.

Demographic trends differ significantly between OECD countries. Figure 2 shows the number of people aged 65 and over compared

---

[69] Luttmer (1998); Alesina & Glaeser (2004).

[70] United Nations (2006).

FIGURE 2. RATIO OF THE POPULATION AGED 65
AND OVER TO THE LABOUR FORCE IN OECD COUNTRIES[71]

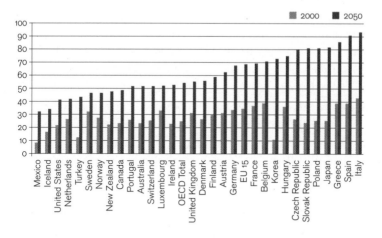

Source: OECD

with the labour force—with today's definition of working age—in
the OECD in the year 2000 and 2050. In some countries, there will be
almost as many people over 65 as there are people in the labour
force. In others, the 65+ share will be a mere 30–50 per cent. Italy,
Spain and Greece are at the top end and Mexico, Iceland and the US
at the end with a small share of 65+. This is not because people do
not live long in these countries but because more children are born
there and there are more immigrants.

With the current definition of working age and retirement age, there
will be a decreasing amount of working people supporting an
increasing amount of retired people. And despite several studies
showing that we are getting healthier—also at a high age—demand

[71] OECD (2007b).

will increase for high-quality health and elderly care. In this scenario, taxes would have to rise. A mandatory retirement age effectively works as a high tax on older workers: if you continue working you will lose pension benefits from the state. That benefits neither employment nor wealth creation. Moreover, evidence suggests that pay-as-you go pension systems (which working people today pay to the retired, instead of the retired having saved in pension accounts themselves) have been negative for private saving and growth rates.[72] To this may be added new values and impulses among people, such as declining faith that the state alone will provide people's pensions, a demand for flexibility, a desire among elderly people for active lives and the rejection by people today of mandatory retirement age.[73]

The demographic situation thus gives rise to a need for reform. Competition in welfare services might help improve productivity and thereby get more services for the money. Freer pensions age, where people who retire later would get higher pensions, would increase incentives to work longer. Things can also be done to make older workers more employable.[74] Switching to more funded pension systems would relieve the potential load on tomorrow's working people. Increasing the share of pensions, health care and elderly care that is privately funded—thereby increasing choice, funding, competition and reflecting personal preferences—is also a long-term strategy for to improve the situation.

A decade ago, there was considerable pessimism about whether countries would be to carry out necessary reforms, mainly in respect of pensions. It is controversial indeed for politicians to cut entitle-

---

[72] Ehrlich & Jinyoung (2005).

[73] HSBC (2007).

[74] OECD (2006c).

ments. But analyses show that things are now happening. Germany, Japan and Sweden have indexed their pension systems to the new demographic reality. Australia has introduced funded pensions and Sweden has personal retirement accounts. Germany, Italy and Spain are trying to introduce more voluntary private pension systems.[75] Reforms of outdated and harmful systems are thus taking place. But while it is encouraging that reforms have been initiated, many countries need to do a great deal more.

Technology

Technological forces have always played an important role in progress. Railways once revolutionised communications, electricity transformed industry and everyday life, and the computer has created enormous gains in communication and efficiency. Inventors have always needed freedom, funding and property rights. And the degree to which countries and societies adopt new technologies depends partly on their openness and the degree of competition. In today's world, technology is a main force behind globalisation itself, as well as the generally increased speed of change. This is due not least to the amount of people that are now part of global business, research and development. The old goods, services, means of production and organisation are changed by technology, while jobs are being constantly replaced by machines and computers.

"Moore's Law" stated that computer power doubles every 18 months (this is now down to every 12 months). Ever more resources are dedicated to research and development, especially in China and India. The cost of mass-producing technological goods falls by some

---

[75] Capretta (2007).

50 per cent a year. In 1968, the price of one transistor was \$1; in 2002 you got 10,000,000 transistors for \$1. The introduction of new technology in society is also quicker. It took 25 years for telephones to reach 25 per cent of the population in the United States, but only 7 years for the Internet to reach the same share.

Research itself is also quicker. It took 15 years to crack the genetic structure of HIV but only 31 days to do the same with the SARS virus.[76] Numerous attempts have been made to predict how technology will change the future, with the limits that predictions always have. One main trend that is commonly cited is the path towards "singularity".[77] This convergence is likely to make the exponential curve of knowledge, communication and development even sharper. It contains principles like a vast increase in computer power, rate of change, communication, merger of human and machine intelligence, and facilitated information sharing.

It is important to note that the development towards singularity is exponential—with 2 billion years from the origins of life to single-celled organisms and just 14 years from the PC to the World Wide Web. The speed of development seems to double every decade. This means that 100 years of progress will be achieved in 25 years measured at the pace of today's progress.[78] During the entire 21st century we will experience the equivalent of 20,000 years of progress at today's speed. One indication of the trend to singularity might be Wikipedia, which is one example of the collective and voluntary knowledge that has been made possible by the new technology. Dis-

---

[76] Ehrenkrona (2006).

[77] At www.kurzweilai.net, there is a vast amount of information and analysis of technological trends and their impact on the future.

[78] Kurzweil (2005).

tance will most likely matter even less in the future, as transaction costs decrease further. A car today is made in hundreds of places all over the world if all the components are taken into account. Production can still be managed even as components are being made wherever conditions are the most suitable.

Technological development is also revolutionising health, with groundbreaking pharmaceuticals being developed and innovations such as keyhole surgery and telecom medication. Research into nanotechnology offers promise, with enthusiasts claiming that in years there will be tiny robots capable of curing a range of human diseases. In robotics, there is a development towards robots performing personal services, which might also be something for future elderly care. Energy is also a sector where technological developments will be of great importance, particularly in increasing energy efficiency and developing new energy sources. Historically, we have abandoned old energy sources before they run out because we have found new sources.[79]

But threats to such a promising technological development do exist, or at least threats that may decrease its speed. One meta-threat is fear of the future and high risk aversion, leading to legislation demanding that no negative outcomes will be allowed from any research—the so-called precautionary principle. Since research is by nature about seeking the new and unknown, the only consequence of adopting that principle broadly will be a reduction in research. Another threat is that there is a tendency to let science become a mere deliverer of pre-determined policies—that scientific conclusions are adapted to political correctness rather than vice versa. Other threats may include poor protection for intellectual property, which is harm-

---

[79] Norberg (2006).

ful to research and development, or government centralising control over research funding. Society's institutions need to have incentives to adopt new technologies. Research and technological development needs similar conditions as other parts of society. There has to be freedom for innovators, trade, competition, seeking funding and profit.

Summary and Conclusions

Society is dynamic and ever-changing. Development is based on the implementation of myriad separate ideas, efforts and actions. In today's increasingly globalised world, more people create more change than ever before. The success stories are numerous, but a society has to open up and embrace change to reap the full benefit. Demographics create a need for reform of welfare services and social security systems. And rapid technological progress, holding promises of wide-ranging improvements for mankind, makes many old systems obsolete. Societies that adapt new technology fast will benefit the most.

DIRECTION OF REFORM AND REFORM AREAS

"To give up the task of reforming society is to give up one's responsibility as a free man."

ALAN PATON

"He who rejects change is the architect of decay. The only human institution which rejects progress is the cemetery."

HAROLD WILSON

EVERY COUNTRY CAN IMPROVE. OECD countries can learn from each other. And long-term trends contribute to a need for reform. But how differently do OECD countries actually perform in important areas? Which ones perform well and which are less successful? How substantial is the need for reform? Which countries have the biggest needs for change? In which areas has a lot been done and where has only a little happened? Which are the most common and well-established reform proposals? The purpose of this chapter is to provide facts about how OECD countries perform, describe the policy conclusions of poor or good performance, and show which reforms are commonly referred to as solutions. This is the story of the need for reform and its consequences, theme by theme.

In recent years, a number of publications have analysed the main problems in rich countries and made policy recommendations. They describe the case for reform in fairly similar ways.[80] Behind all these figures, diagrams and tables there is a reality of real people and real lives—and it is the real world which is important. All the same, data provide the best way of having reliable results and conclusions that do not rely solely on anecdotes, storytelling or single observations, however catchy they may be.

A framework for an assessment of the need for reform is the concept of economic freedom, as formulated in the annual "Index of Economic Freedom" studies published by the Heritage Foundation and Wall Street Journal. In 2007, it was published for the 13th consecutive year and measured the degree of economic freedom in 157 countries. The analysis is based on objective data from, for example, the OECD and the World Bank and looks at ten categories—in turn based on a large number of indicators. The ten categories are: business, trade, fiscal, government size, monetary, investment, financial, property, corruption and labour. In each category, the degree of freedom for economic exchange is assessed on a scale from 1 to 100.[81]

Like any country comparison or index, it is a simplification. However, the index is used by governments over the world and is, after 13 years of debate, refined and respected all over the world. It also says something important about reality. The degree of economic freedom in a country is closely correlated to the level of GDP per capita. Most countries have increased their economic freedom during the last decade, and those that have made the most substantial increases have also increased their growth rates the most. There is also a correlation between a high degree of economic freedom and low unemployment.

---

[80] For example, OECD (2007a); Sapir (2003); Baily & Farrell (2005); Alesina & Giavazzi (2006).

[81] Kane, Holmes & O'Grady (2007).

FIGURE 3. ECONOMIC FREEDOM AND GDP PER CAPITA,
OECD COUNTRIES.[82]

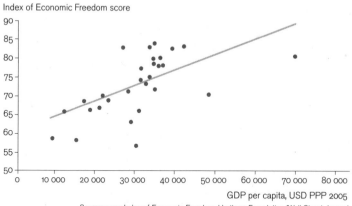

Source: 2007 Index of Economic Freedom, Heritage Foundation/Wall Street Journal.

The methodology is not designed to recommend that a country should have no regulations or no taxes to have a full score; it is a matter of degrees. Contrary to other published indexes, this is clearly not just a theoretical product without relevance to reality. For example, the Global Competitiveness Report by the World Economic Forum shows no correlation between a country's position and its growth rate for the past years.[83] In such a case, one has to question the report's definition of the term "competitiveness" and indeed the relevance of the index itself. The general direction of reform—if one desires prosperity—should thus be towards more economic freedom. This chapter describes OECD countries' performance in areas of importance for economic success, that is, the main areas that comprise the concept of economic freedom.

---

[82] GDP per capita is USD, PPP, 2005, Index of Economic Freedom is the 2007 edition, where the analysis is based on data in different categories from different years—to a large extent 2004, 2005 and 2006.

[83] World Economic Forum (2007).

Growth

Growth is the overall consequence of an efficiently working economy and has many causes. It is not just a figure on paper. GDP per
capita, for instance, is closely correlated over time with the proportion of children born who survive their first year. Conversely, a
factor such as the degree of public health care funding, is, perhaps
surprisingly, not correlated to the share of children that survive their
first year.[84] Growth is important, but several OECD countries have
had low growth rates for a long time. This is not something that
changes with an economic boom that lasts for a few years. In the
short run, a difference between growth rates of 3 per cent or 5 per
cent might seem small, but in the longer run it determines whether
incomes will double in 23 or 15 years. This is why achieving sustained growth is the main economic policy objective for most national
governments, political parties and international organisations like
the OECD, the IMF and the EU.

The global economy grew by 3.3 per cent on average annually in
1980–2000 and by 4.2 per cent on average in 2000–2006. The growth
rates for low income countries were even higher.[86] The projections
point to a global growth level over 4 per cent every year until 2012.[87]
The GDP of China today is about 700 per cent higher than in 1980,
while India's is 400 per cent higher.[88] Never before have so many
people been part of the global workforce, and still there are hundreds
of millions of people on their way. Real wages in the EU-15 increased
by 1.1 per cent annually on average in 1991–2000 and are predicted

---

[84] World Health Organization (a).

[85] IMF Database, October 2007.

[86] The World Bank (2006b).

[87] IMF (2007).

[88] OECD, Central Statistical Organisation of India.

to rise by 0.9 per cent annually in 2000–2008. In the US, the equivalent figures are 1.6 and 1.9 per cent.[89]

One way to describe the components of economic growth is to look at hours worked and productivity during those hours. The more hours worked, and the more value produced per hour, the higher is GDP per capita. The number of hours worked in the economy can increase by having a larger number of people working, or working more hours per person. Productivity can rise for a number of reasons, such as IT and technology use, investment and rationalisation, competition, and increased skills. In the long run, what really determines prosperity is productivity growth—when a country climbs up the productivity ladder.

Today, average European GDP per capita is about 70 per cent of GDP per capita in the United States. The difference can be attributed to the following factors, in roughly equal measure: fewer hours worked per person; a smaller share of the population working; and lower productivity.[90] This has not changed, except slightly in the opposite direction, compared to 2000, when EU leaders agreed to close the gap with the US by 2010. Productivity growth in the US was almost twice the rate of that in the 15 EU countries in 1995–2004, largely due to very low productivity in the EU services sector and poor use of IT.[91]

Figure 4 shows the levels of Gross Domestic Product per capita in the OECD countries in 2005. It can provide an image of the current situation in terms of which countries are the wealthiest and which have lower incomes. Luxembourg, Norway, the US, Switzerland and the

---

[89] European Commission (2006b).

[90] Sapir (2003).

[91] EU KLEMS Database (2007).

FIGURE 4. GROSS DOMESTIC PRODUCT PER CAPITA,
OECD COUNTRIES, 2005.

Adjusted for purchasing power, USD

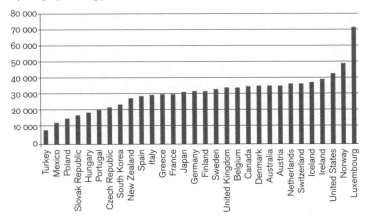

Source: OECD

Netherlands are at the top. Turkey, Mexico, Poland, the Slovak Republic and Hungary are at the bottom. This is the current situation—not the direction of development.

Why do fewer Europeans work? And when they do, why do they work less and produce less value than Americans? There are substantial differences between European countries, but this pattern is true of most of Western Europe. The degree of employment has a great deal to do with the institutions of the labour market. High minimum wages—either imposed by law or by collective bargaining—lead to a situation where low-productive people are employed to a lower degree. High taxes on work and high levels of public social contributions to those who do not work, possible to receive for a very long time, create disincentives against working. Strict mandatory retirement ages have the same effect.[92]

The reason for working fewer hours is similar. It has been claimed that Europeans simply value leisure more. But looking at the actual incentives against working more, such as progressive and high income taxes, a lot more suggests that Europeans are rational and follow incentives.[93] One study has also "leisure-adjusted" GDP levels—partly by looking at spending on leisure activities—and found that Americans value leisure at least as much as Europeans do.[94] Lastly, why are productivity rates developing poorly in many, though not all, Western European countries? Common explanations include regulated product markets, small domestic markets for companies, regulated labour markets and, again, poor incentives to work.[95] Reforms to raise productivity levels should thus focus on deregulation, openness to trade, freeing up the labour market and increasing incentives to work. Comparative studies have found that countries with broad private ownership have higher productivity growth and that slow productivity growth is linked to extensive regulation of businesses.[96]

Competition is essential for economic and societal development. It is the driving force behind the development of better and cheaper goods and services and new and more efficient ways to organise companies. A study of 3,300 firms in 25 transition countries showed that increased competition increased sales and labour productivity

---

[92] OECD (2007a).

[93] Alesina & Giavazzi (2006).

[94] OECD Observer (2006).

[95] Baily & Farrell (2006).

[96] Phelps (1997).

and desire to develop new products.[97] It has been estimated that about half the difference in prosperity between the United States and the euro-zone can be explained by less competition in the euro-zone.[98] That is, restrictions on competition are responsible for several thousand euro in lower annual income for the average European—and still, the United States could also benefit from more competition in several areas.

In recent decades OECD countries have introduced reliable macro-economic frameworks. In monetary policy, low inflation guaranteed by independent central banks, has become the norm. In fiscal policy, keeping deficits limited (some countries even aim for surpluses) has replaced the idea of deliberately having deficits to make the effects of recessions somewhat smoother. The process of launching reforms to introduce these frameworks was a consequence of serious economic problems in many OECD countries in the 1970s, with high inflation, large deficits and high unemployment. The process has been step-wise, with the 1990s as the intensive period when many important decisions were taken. Several of the steps, such as aiming for low information and making central banks independent, were controversial and were launched amid political battles. They are much more generally accepted as frameworks for economic policy today. Achieving this macroeconomic stabilisation has contributed to better economic performance in the OECD and to a stronger focus on the need for microeconomic reforms.

Real GDP growth—the annual percentage increase on average between 1992 and 2005—is shown in Figure 5. The countries with the top growth rates are not the same as those with the highest levels of

---

[97] Carlin et al (2001).

[98] Bayoumi, Laxton & Pesenti (2004).

FIGURE 5. GROWTH OF GDP, OECD COUNTRIES, 1996–2005.
Annual percentage growth, average

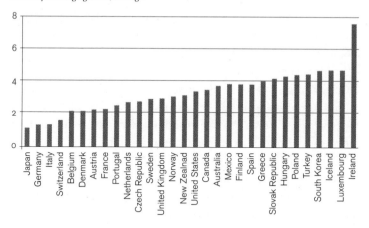

Source: OECD

prosperity today, as shown in Figure 2, which indicates that countries will continue to change places. A poor but strongly growing country might remain largely poor for several years, just as some wealthy countries grow fast. Ireland, Luxembourg, Iceland, the US and Australia are already at the top half of the current prosperity level and have high growth rates. Hence, there are countries that seem to defend their position and continue to grow strongly despite the fact that they are already wealthy. And that is a sign of the potential for growth-enhancing reforms in the other countries with lower growth rates.

Incomes, Wealth and Poverty

GDP per capita is one measure of income per person and year but does not take the distribution of income into account. If the wealthy have everything and the poor nothing, the average income per person would look all right. One first point is that living standards are not just determined by incomes, but also by wealth. Some countries actually have high incomes but low wealth. The Luxembourg Wealth Study analysed seven industrialised countries and concluded that average private personal wealth differs substantially between wealthy nations, with median private wealth of about €120,000 in Italy and only €20,000 in Sweden. The countries in between, in ascending order, are the UK, Finland, the US, Canada and Germany.[99] Italians might therefore be able to afford better living standards than their levels of annual income would indicate.

Another measure to take into account when studying incomes could be the annual private consumption per person. That is the average amount that a person spends in a year, after taxes and net savings have been deducted and contributions received. In the US, annual private consumption is the highest in the OECD—more than €25,000. The other top countries are Luxembourg, the UK, Switzerland and Austria. The OECD countries with the lowest private consumption are Turkey, Mexico and Poland, at about €4,000–6,000, largely reflecting their still low GDP levels. But some countries have high GDP per capita but their private consumption still only ranks in the lower half, at about €12,000, like Finland and Sweden, reflecting high taxes and thus high levels of public consumption.[100]

Figure 6 shows how the disposable income is distributed among the population, using the so-called Gini coefficient. Zero level means that everyone has the same income; 100 means that the poorest have nothing and the wealthy have all the income. Income differentials are widest in Mexico, Turkey, Poland and the US, and narrowest in

---

[99] Luxembourg Income Study (2006).
[100] OECD.

FIGURE 6. DISTRIBUTION OF HOUSEHOLD DISPOSABLE INCOME
AMONG INDIVIDUALS, OECD COUNTRIES.[101]

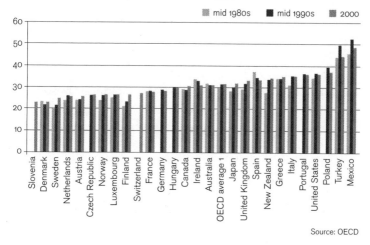

Source: OECD

Denmark, Sweden, the Netherlands and Austria. Though there are
differentials between countries, the situation has remained the same
within countries in recent decades (apart from minor changes). In
many countries where the differentials are very small, the income
levels before taxes and public contributions are larger. The state
actively uses taxes and contributions to narrow differentials.

How have disposable incomes developed during the last decade?
They have increased, to a particularly large degree in Eastern and
Central Europe. But incomes stagnated or even went into reverse in
Continental Europe and Japan. Interestingly, the disposable incomes
of those 10 per cent with the lowest incomes have performed in line
with the average in every country. In a few countries, their incomes
have performed slightly worse, and in a few countries their incomes

---

[101] OECD Statistical Database (2000).

FIGURE 7. GROWTH OF DISPOSABLE INCOME 1995–2004 FOR
THE WHOLE POPULATION AND FOR THE 10 PER CENT WITH
THE LOWEST INCOMES, CURRENT PRICES, US$.[102]

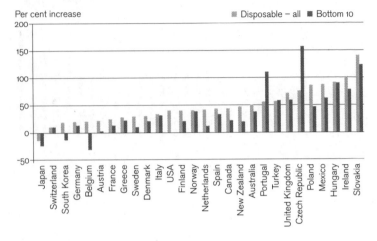

Source: Euromonitor

have clearly outperformed the average. This largely reflects economic growth rates during the same period.

What about actual poverty? Relative income differentials constitute
one relevant aspect, and poverty is another. A country can have very
small income differentials yet widespread poverty if average income
is very low, as in North Korea. And a country can have large income
differentials but reasonable living standards for the poorest if average income is high, as in Ireland. An absolute measure—actual
income in euro or dollars—is a way to see actual standards for
people including those on low incomes. After all, living standards
are determined by what you can actually afford to buy, not a relative

---

[102] Euromonitor International (2006).

FIGURE 8. SHARE OF HOUSEHOLDS WITH A POST-TAX INCOME BELOW $20,000 A YEAR IN 1990 AND 2004 AT CURRENT PRICES, US $.[103]

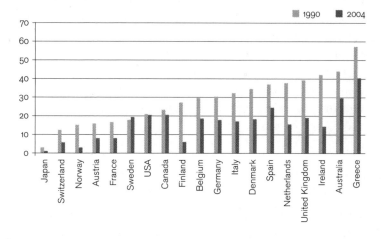

Source: Euromonitor

position compared to anyone else. Sometimes, a figure might seem to suggest that incomes for a certain group have stagnated, but the reason can be that new people are added and others leave the group. In the United States, for example, average incomes might at times seem to stand still. However, a typical male worker with some college education but no degree has seen a pay rise from $34,000 to $40,000 since 2000.[104]

Euromonitor has analysed how the household share of the population with a net income below $20,000 a year in a number of countries has developed. Between 1990 and 2004, it decreased in all the

---

[103] Euromonitor International (2006).

[104] Brooks (2006).

analysed countries except Sweden, where there was a slight increase. Countries like Ireland, Finland, the UK and the Netherlands had a quite large share of households with low incomes in 1990 but have managed to decrease that share drastically. In the United States—not included in the diagram above—the share of households that make less than $75,000 a year has decreased by 14 per cent in the past 25 years.[105] These are also countries that have seen strong economic and employment growth in the wake of reforms. These facts naturally underline the social argument for implementing reform: incomes rise and poverty decreases.

Jobs

Which areas of society, then, are the most relevant for reform to achieve better performance and, ultimately, rising growth, incomes and living standards? How do OECD countries perform in these different areas? Where are there substantial problems, where have reforms been launched, and with what results?

First, employment is rightly at the centre of economic analysis and debate. Having a job is of great importance to any individual and increasing people's opportunities to get a job must be a leading social aim. Employment is also essential for society as a whole, since production of goods and services is the essence of wealth creation. Unemployment, especially long-term and for young people, can come at a huge cost with social unrest, crime and riots as consequences. A main source of a person's social security is the knowledge that he or she will be able to support himself or herself. Many people who can work do not get the chance.

---

[105] Brooks (2006).

FIGURE 9. TOTAL EMPLOYMENT IN OECD COUNTRIES 2005
(SHARE OF PERSONS OF WORKING AGE, 15–64, IN
EMPLOYMENT).[106]

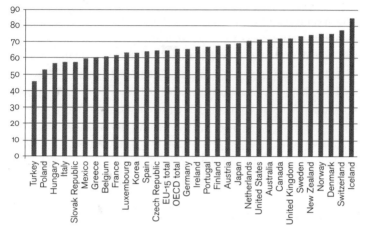

Source: OECD

Employment rates differ significantly between OECD countries. The total employment rate ranges from 45.9 per cent in Turkey to 84.4 per cent in Iceland. Clearly, quite a number of countries have great potential for increasing employment. Of course there are differences in how to classify employed people from country to country. People on sick leave, maternity leave or even unemployed in government labour programmes are sometimes referred to as employed. In particular, the unemployed may be called something else where there are a lot of public social and employment programmes. So the real levels of people actually working might be slightly different. In several cases, a couple of percentage points should probably be deducted from the

---

[106] OECD (2006).

official figures. But that does not alter the existence of big differentials or remove the potential for improvement. On the contrary.

Which countries have been the most successful in increasing employment rates in recent years? The differences, shown in Figure 10, are substantial. Some have experienced a fall in employment, whereas some have had a tremendous increase. The development of the country's population is an underlying factor. A country with an increasing population will probably find it easier to increase the number of employed. There is no apparent evidence of the strong employment growth in some countries being only catch-up in nature. Some countries that already had high employment rates a decade ago have also experienced a strong continued increase, like New Zealand, Australia, Iceland and the UK. So there is no limit to improvement—and starting at a low level is no guarantee of improvement.

FIGURE 10. EMPLOYMENT GROWTH, OECD COUNTRIES 1996–2006.

Total percentage change

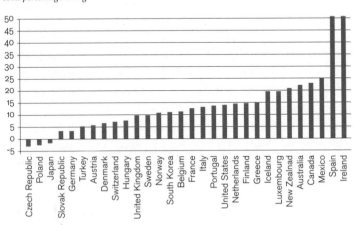

Source: OECD

Unemployment, then, is largely the flip-side of employment. But countries with the lowest employment rates do not necessarily have the highest unemployment rates. After all, you are only unemployed if you actively look and apply for a job. In some countries, there is more of a tradition that some individuals are supported by the family and are neither considered employed nor employed. There are other groups, too, that are considered to be neither. Countries define unemployment in widely differing ways, but the official figures indicate the main pattern. Seventeen of the 30 OECD countries have official unemployment rates of 7 per cent or below and the rest are below 10 per cent (except Poland and the Slovak Republic, which have very high levels of 16–17 per cent).

Employment and unemployment among young people (those aged 15–24) differs even more. In Iceland, Australia, Denmark and the Netherlands, over 60 per cent of that group is employed, but in Poland, Hungary, Greece, Luxembourg and Italy fewer than 30 per cent are. This also largely reflects which countries which have high and low youth unemployment. Long-term unemployment means people who have been unemployed for 12 months or more as a share of the total unemployment. It is highest—over half of total unemployment—in the Slovak Republic, Germany, Greece and the Czech Republic and lowest (less than 10 per cent of total unemployment) in South Korea, Mexico, New Zealand and Norway.[107]

In which major ways to the institutions and policies differ? Why are some successful and some not? And which reforms would be necessary to improve employment?

---

[107] OECD (2007b).

The state makes numerous interventions in the labour market and those interventions have effects. A large share of the workforce has the state as employer; there are taxes that affect the price of hiring and the profitability of work; regulations may determine how, where, when and how much a person is allowed to work; and social security systems provide support for many people who are—for various reasons—not working. The World Bank makes an annual assessment of this in its Doing Business Index, and in the 2007 Index of Economic Freedom the various categories from the Doing Business Index are added together in a list where 100 is a high degree of freedom in the labour market and zero is a very high degree of regulation.[108]

FIGURE 11. LABOUR FREEDOM IN OECD COUNTRIES.

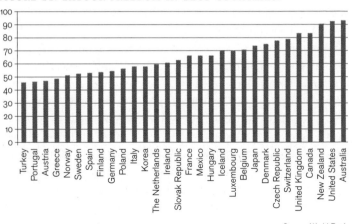

Source: World Bank

The chart shows there are great differences between OECD countries when it comes to labour market institutions and policies. A comparison with the charts showing employment levels and employment

---

[108] Details at http://www.doingbusiness.org/ExploreTopics/EmployingWorkers/

growth in different countries indicates a correlation with the degree of labour market freedom. The higher the degree of labour market freedom, the higher employment and employment growth tend to be and vice versa. The top and bottom countries are roughly the same. There are two main exceptions: Ireland and the Netherlands perform well yet have a fairly high degree of intervention in the labour market.

Does this imply that the degree of labour freedom is irrelevant for employment results after all? The answer is no. First, the number of countries where there is an obvious correlation is quite large. Second, both Ireland and the Netherlands have a high degree of economic freedom in most other areas. As has been mentioned, taxes and social security systems also affect the labour market but are not part of this measure. Doing most other things right will have a positive effect on employment too. This should, however, not be interpreted as an argument that one good reform can compensate for a bad one; two good reforms will always produce the best results.

Numerous studies can provide evidence that a large degree of labour market regulation leads to lower employment and higher unemployment. The OECD, for example, has published a number of studies which have provided part of the basis for the analysis and recommendations in the "OECD Jobs Strategy".[109] Why regulation creates unemployment can be described by simple and all too common examples from reality. If the state makes it hard to fire someone, for example by law, this makes employers more reluctant to hire people for the simple reason that a recruitment mistake cannot be easily corrected. If working hours are regulated, companies that need flexible working hours (for example those dependent on the season) will

---

[109] Such studies include, for example, Nicoletti & Scarpetta (2005); Bassanini & Duval (2006); OECD (2006a).

think twice before hiring. If a tax that doubles the price of hiring is imposed, it might become too expensive for many entrepreneurs to take people on.

There may be different reasons for governments to intervene in the labour market, such as making the labour more efficient, gaining political power or a consequence of the legal system. One study found that the labour market is actually made more inefficient and also found evidence both of governments seeking more political power and correlations with the type of legal system.[110] A government basing parts of its political power on labour market regulation will find it difficult to reform the labour market. In the public debate, of course, the main argument for intervention is the protection of workers against social insecurity. The effect however seems to be the opposite, as shown in Figure 12.

The OECD Employment Outlook from 2004 contains evidence which suggests that worker uncertainty increases when employment protection legislation (EPL) is stricter.[112] There may be several explanations for this. Ironically, strict labour market regulations might produce a double uncertainty. First, among those who have a job and fear losing it, and second among those who do not have a job and find it very hard to get one. There is evidence suggesting that strict labour market regulations might lead to "Prozac economics". In other words, people in companies facing a downturn where the labour market is more

---

[110] Botero et al (2004).

[112] There is also a correlation in the 2004 OECD Employment Outlook showing that more generous unemployment benefits make employees feel more secure. This might seem perfectly logical but it does not say anything about the effects of such benefits on labour costs, employment or working incentives. And it does not distinguish between public or private systems for unemployment benefits.

FIGURE 12. STRICT LABOUR MARKET REGULATION INCREASES WORKER INSECURITY[111]

Security index for employees on permanent contracts, late 1990s

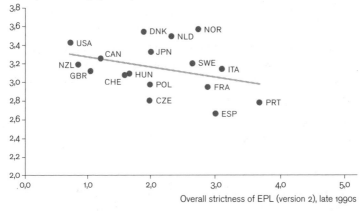

Overall strictness of EPL (version 2), late 1990s

Source: OECD

regulated might get pressured to quit voluntarily, experience high stress levels and consume more medication to relieve the pressure.[113]

The labour market not only contains employees, employers and the state. The so-called social partners are also important features of any labour market, the main stakeholders being the organisations of employers and employees. They are often partly integrated in the system of state labour market intervention, for example by administering unemployment benefits, co-deciding on labour market matters or *de facto* setting minimum wages by far-reaching collective bargaining. Countries that have a fairly low degree of state labour market regulation sometimes have powerful trade unions instead.

---

[111] OECD (2004).

[113] Wasmer (2006).

With the stated aim of preventing "social dumping", trade unions work to raise wages, particularly minimum wages. Trade unions might contribute to higher wage increases in the short term, but in the long term productivity development is the most important factor. Real wages have been rising at least as rapidly in countries where collective bargaining coverage is very limited. And the wage share of the total economy is at least as big in several countries where few people belong to trade unions as it is in countries where many belong to unions.[114] France and Sweden are highly unionised and have experienced lower increases in real wages than countries like the UK, where very few are covered by collective bargaining.[115] Raising minimum wages might lead to unemployment among people with low productivity. The theory of "insiders and outsiders" is a tool that explains many labour market regulations and trade union powers, despite the adverse effects on employment.[116]

In most OECD countries, a majority of people in employment work in the service sector.[117] There are differences, with some countries well above 70 per cent and others below 50 per cent. In several of these countries, a large share of service production takes place in the public sector. As the share of people working in manufacturing industry has decreased, the number of people producing services has increased. It should be remembered that industrial production has continued to increase; it is just that manufacturing does not require as many employees any more, not least thanks to technical progress. A high share of people producing services is correlated with low unemployment and high GDP per capita.[118] The transition to a more

---

[114] European Commission (2006b).

[115] OECD (2004b).

[116] An overview is provided in Lindbeck & Snower (2002).

[117] OECD (2007b).

[118] The World bank (2007a)

service-oriented society should therefore be facilitated: the old jobs must go and new ones come in. This emphasises the need for reforms like reductions in labour and income taxes, since services normally are more labour-intensive than manufacturing.

A number of reform recommendations are commonly cited for OECD countries.[119] There is evidence that "in-work benefit" reforms—for example lower taxes for employed people—have a strong positive result for labour supply.[120] A number of developments have been seen in the last ten years, especially the creation of a better macroeconomic framework with a monetary policy for low inflation and a fiscal policy with a better budgetary balance. But a number of issues remain to be resolved, according to established analyses. These include cutting payroll taxes, cutting income taxes—particularly for low-income earners, liberalising job security laws, deregulating product markets, reducing wage rigidities, increasing incentives to work, replacing passive income support with activity support and modernising job training.

Taxes

Every state collects taxes. Citizens have to pay taxes, whether they use certain public services or not. Taxes are the main way of funding expenditures that society considers appropriate to bear collectively. What should be paid for and delivered on a voluntary basis in the private sphere of society, and what should be mandatory and thus tax-funded, is an ideological and political question. The current situation in OECD countries is the result of an incremental development

---

[119] For example in the OECD (2006a).

[120] Immervoll et al (2004).

over a long period of time and in which numerous stakeholders have had a role. It is by no means a result of a single clear thought followed through. There is great potential for improving and simplifying tax systems.

Where and how individual taxes are collected will affect society and its development. Indeed, that is often the intention of taxes: high taxes on tobacco and alcohol in many countries aim to reduce people's consumption of these goods. The effects of taxes depend on how price-sensitive different goods and services are, which is a matter of considerable study among researchers and public officials. Naturally, when the state collects taxes it will also use the money in a way that is different from what would otherwise have happened—and that too has an effect. Public spending replaces private spending, euro by euro, dollar by dollar.

FIGURE 13. TOTAL TAX REVENUE AS A SHARE OF GDP
IN OECD COUNTRIES, 2004[121]

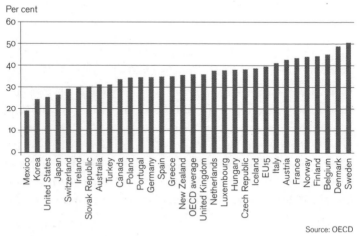

Source: OECD

---

[121] OECD (2007b).

Figure 13 shows total tax revenue in OECD countries. Total tax revenue means adding all the revenues from individual taxes—income taxes, corporate taxes, energy taxes, etc—together and comparing the sum with the total national GDP. The highest taxes in the world can be found in Northern and Western Europe, whereas North America and Eastern and Central Europe generally have substantially lower taxes. In 1965, the span of tax pressure in OECD countries ranged from 15 per cent to 35 per cent of GDP. In 2005, the span was 27 per cent to 51 per cent.[122] The more decades one were to go back in time prior to 1965, the greater the divergence would be with circumstances today. The further back you go, the lower taxes were. This shows how substantial the increase has been during this rather limited period.

Increases in some countries have been less dramatic than in others. For example, US tax pressure has remained roughly the same, while some countries—notably Ireland and Luxembourg—have actually seen a substantial drop in tax pressure during the last 20 years. But generally speaking, tax pressure has risen. For most countries, however, the level seems to have come to a halt during the last decade or two. One study concluded: "Pressures for more spending are now clearly recognised as coming from vested interests rather than from the public interest."[123] It should also be noted that GDP has increased in these 40 years, so a doubling of the tax pressure did not imply a doubling of revenue (revenue increased much more). The growth of the public sector has thus been more substantial than the mere increase in total taxes.

Figure 14 shows the total labour and income tax bill that low-income earners—people with an income of 67 per cent of the national average

---

[122]   OECD; Karlson (2004).

[123]   Tanzi & Schuknecht (1997).

—have to pay. In quite a number of OECD countries taxes account for more than 40 per cent of the wage cost. It is true that in many countries, these people get a lot back from the state, but it is also true that they do pay a lot. This not only determines how much people with already low incomes can keep after tax; it also affects how profitable it is to go to work and how expensive it is to hire them. A large number of the countries that have been successful in raising employment are found in the lower half, with low taxes for low-income earners.

FIGURE 14. AVERAGE PERSONAL INCOME TAX AND SOCIAL SECURITY CONTRIBUTION RATES ON GROSS LABOUR INCOME FOR LOW-INCOME EARNERS, OECD COUNTRIES, 2006[124]

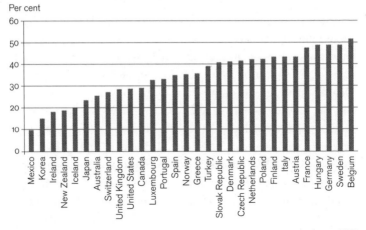

Per cent

Source: OECD

The rise in tax pressure has coincided with lower economic growth and higher unemployment for many countries, in particular in Western Europe. As mentioned, public officials study closely how

---

[124] OECD Statistical Database (2000).

individual taxes affect economic activity in different sectors. One study concludes that the increase in taxes on labour in Europe 1965–1991 explains a third of the lower growth and created a rise in unemployment by four percentage points during that period.[125] There is a discussion about the size of the effects on growth by the total tax pressure, as well as a discussion about how to collect the taxes in the simplest way.[126] There is also a debate about the magnitude of the effects of labour taxes on the level of employment.[127] Individual taxes matter, but it seems that the total level of taxes—all else equal—does too.[128] There is, for example, evidence that decisions by corporations about where to invest in the European Union are more affected by an assessment of the whole tax burden, not least on labour, than just the corporate tax rate.[129]

There are countries that have experienced high growth and a positive development of employment despite high tax pressures. To a large extent, these countries have launched other, compensating, reforms. Over time, it has become harder for governments to collect taxes, since tax bases have become more mobile. Capital and corporate taxes have decreased in most OECD countries. Instead, less mobile tax bases like consumption, people on low incomes, and property are taxed. But income taxes are coming down too nowadays, with low and flat taxes spreading. Particularly in the enlarged European Union, with 27 member countries, there is a tax competition that creates a race

---

[125] Daveri & Tabellini (1997).

[126] Katz (2006).

[127] Hansson (2006).

[128] A selection of studies that have analysed the effects of taxes on economic activity might be Tanzi, Vito; Zee (1996); Ahmed (1986), Fu, Taylor & Yücel (2003); Davis & Henrekson (2005); Abrams (1999); Bassanini & Scarpetta (2001); Engen & Skinner (1992); Alesina et al (1999); Tanzi & Schuknecht (1996), Karras (1996), Carlstrom & Gokhale (1991).

[129] De Santis, Mercuri & Vicarelli (2001).

TABLE 2. FLAT-TAX JURISDICTIONS, 2007[130]

Country	Year of Enactment	Tax Rate
Jersey	1940	20%
Hong Kong	1947	16%
Guernsey	1960	20%
Estonia	1994	22%
Latvia	1995	25%
Lithuania	1996	27%
Russia	2001	13%
Serbia	2003	14%
Slovakia	2004	19%
Ukraine	2004	15%
Romania	2005	16%
Georgia	2005	12%
Iceland	2007	35.7%
Mongolia	2007	10%
Kyrgyzstan	2007	10%
Macedonia	2007	12%
Future Flat Tax Jurisdictions		
Montenegro	2007 (July)	15%
Mauritius	2009	15%
Active Consideration		
Albania	2008	10%
Czech Republic	2008	15%

Source: Mitchell, Daniel J

---

[130] Mitchell (2007).

to the top in terms of decreasing and simplifying taxes in creating the best climate for investments, corporations, education and work.

Taxes are one area where there is extensive pressure to reform—to make them simpler and lower—and where many changes are currently under way. The current global and European tax competition is in fact a race to the top in improving conditions for growth, employment and rising living standards. Taxes do affect a country's attractiveness in a global market and indeed the profitability of taking risks, going through education, working more, starting a company or making investments.[131] High taxes can lead to lower revenue—as when Sweden raised tobacco taxes substantially in 1997—and lower taxes can lead to higher revenue—as when Ireland cut corporate tax. Thus, if lower taxes boost growth, there might not be a need to reduce public expenditure by as much as the tax cut. People and companies will not remain indifferent if taxes are cut. Incentives work.

Social Security

Social safety is very important to most people. We are exposed to different risks and may judge them differently, but most people want to feel secure. This is partly a matter of welfare services; if we get sick, we want access to health care, for example. But it is also very much a matter of ensuring that we have some kind of income if we become unemployed or sick—or when we get older and eventually retire. In most of today's wealthy countries, such social safety systems account for the largest share the public spending. It is not obvious why these systems are public and others are not. Why is home insurance private and unemployment insurance usually public, for example?

---

[131] For an account of the positive effects of tax competition, study Teather (2005).

Why some things are public and some are private is sometimes hard to see. Health care is usually mostly public, but production and retail of medication is not, though it is intensively regulated. Today's public social safety systems have several problems, such as lack of choice for citizens and thereby lack of competition between providers. The fact that these systems account for the largest share of public spending explains a large part of the high taxes, with their often problematic effects. There is thus a need for reform, which also has to take into account some of people's demands in respect of social security.

FIGURE 15. PUBLIC SOCIAL EXPENDITURE,
OECD COUNTRIES, 2003[132]

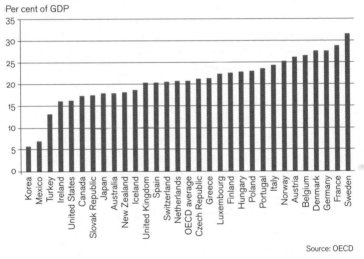

Per cent of GDP

Source: OECD

Total public expenditure is of course largely the flip side of tax pressure; it is what the state does with the taxes it collects. Figure 15 shows public social expenditure levels in the OECD countries as a share of

[132] OECD (2007b).

GDP. These economic transfers—pensions and other social security systems—constitute for most OECD countries the largest share of total public spending. Substantial differences exist between the OECD countries, though most are within the range of 15 percent to 30 per cent. This does not measure which country is more "social" than another, since private social programmes or social insurances are excluded.

The overwhelming majority of these social expenditures are not transfers from one person to another, such as from a person with a high income to a disabled person, but pensions and other social systems with income-related benefits (for example, for sickness or unemployment). That is, most of public social expenditure is received by the same persons that once paid for it. Naturally, some resources are also consumed by administration. A large share of the social spending is received by people who are, for various reasons, not in work. There is evidence from countries that introduced private administration of social insurance systems—in this case, disability insurance in the Netherlands—limiting the duration of people being in the system as well as the number of people entering it, as efforts increased to get people back to work.[133] Welfare services, namely education, health care and elderly care, comprise the other major component of public expenditure but are not part of Figure 10.

Very high public spending implies that the tax pressure has to be high. A country that wants to cut taxes has to look at its public spending. State welfare services and social security systems are subject to a number of internal difficulties. Growing systems for income transfers to people who do not work are crowding out public welfare services. There is also often a lack of choice for citizens in these systems and, by definition, no real competition where the state is the sole provider.

---

[133] Zwinkels, Brouwer & Braat (2006).

Monopolies—private or public—tend to lead to waiting lists, inefficiency, waste and poorer services.

By having these services delivered by public monopolies, there is a risk that they have to be rationed. Studies have shown that people would often be prepared to pay even more to such services than they already have paid in tax.[134] But since the tax pressure cannot rise and would rather have to come down, the belt is tight around these highly demanded services. As the services become more expensive due to lower productivity than goods production, and as the demand rises due to higher incomes and taxes come down, the belt will get ever tighter.[135]

Table 2 shows the degree of efficiency in 23 industrialised countries, according to a study by the European Central Bank. The highest efficiency is 1 and zero is the lowest. Countries at the top thus have very efficient public sectors. Half of these countries could cut public spending by 25 per cent or more and yet have the same output if their public sectors were as efficient as those in the US, Japan or Luxembourg. The study's conclusion is that countries with a more limited public sector have higher efficiency.

A number of OECD countries have cut public spending. Ireland, Belgium, the UK and the Netherlands did so by more than ten percentage points of GDP during the 1980s. Finland, Sweden, Canada and Spain did likewise during the 1990s. Austria, Denmark, New Zealand, the United States, Italy, Japan, Belgium, Germany, France and Switzerland also reduced public spending during the 1980s or 1990s, though by less than five percentage points. The more substan-

---

[134] Fogel (1999).
[135] Baumol (1967), Baumol, Blackman, & Wolff (1985).

TABLE 3. PUBLIC SECTOR EFFICIENCY[136]

Country	Efficiency (1.00 = max)
United States, Japan, Luxembourg	1.00
Australia	0.99
Ireland	0.96
Switzerland	0.95
Iceland	0.87
United Kingdom	0.84
New Zealand	0.83
Spain	0.80
Portugal	0.79
Canada	0.75
Norway, Greece	0.73
Netherlands, Germany	0.72
Austria	0.67
Italy, Belgium	0.66
France	0.64
Denmark	0.62
Finland	0.61
Sweden	0.57

Source: European Central Bank

tial reductions were all part of reform packages that also included reforms such as deregulation, privatisation and tax cuts. The countries that made more ambitious cuts in public spending experienced rather profound improvements in the soundness of the public finances. Furthermore, they had a rather quick improvement of growth and

---

[136] Afonso, Schuknecht & Tanzi (2003).

trend growth rates.[137] Last but not least, the countries that reduced public spending substantially did not experience lower values for socio-economic indicators, such as human development or income distribution.[138]

Health Care

Health is very important to most people. Many things that affect your health are largely part of the private sphere, such as exercise, spa visits, nutrition and many medications. But in most countries, health care provision is largely via the public sector. A main reason for this has been guaranteeing equal access to health care. Since health is important, health care is a service that has a high priority for many people. Studies have shown that people would like to devote all of a possible increase in income to having better health care, if that were possible.[139] Normally, such a strong and rising level of demand for any good or service would lead to a development of the health care supply. But health care is a part of society which, in most countries, has problems relating to access, quality, efficiency and information. Why is health care not a flourishing, dynamic, sector? And what reforms would be necessary to get it there?

Figure 16 shows how much the OECD countries spend per person a year on health care; the year is 2004 for most countries and 2003 for some. The US, Luxembourg and Switzerland spend the most; Turkey, Mexico and the Slovak Republic spend the least. Average public spending as a share of total health care spending is 73 per cent in the

---

[137] Hauptmeier, Heipertz & Schuknecht (2006).

[138] Schuknecht & Tanzi (2005).

[139] Fogel (1999).

FIGURE 16. PUBLIC AND PRIVATE EXPENDITURE
ON HEALTH IN OECD COUNTRIES, US$ PER CAPITA.[140]

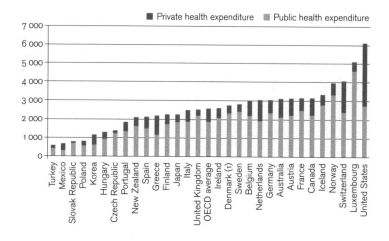

Source: OECD

OECD, with some variation. Public funding consists of taxes and
private funding may come from private insurance, foundations or
fees. In most of Europe, public funding clearly dominates—except in
Switzerland and the Netherlands. The US has higher public spending on health care than most countries, yet the majority of health
care spending is private. Health Consumer Powerhouse attempts
annually to analyse health care from a consumer perspective in different countries in Europe. The results from its 2006 survey are shown
in Figure 17.

The comparability might be a bit limited, due to different selections
of countries. Of course there is a correlation between GDP per capita

---

[140] OECD (2007b).

FIGURE 17. EURO HEALTH CONSUMER INDEX 2007[141]

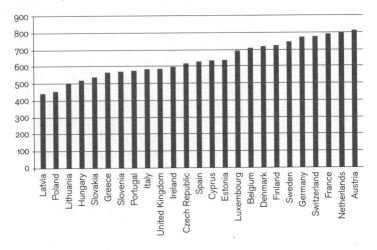

Source: OECD

and health care quality, but there is not a perfect correlation between spending and results. Some countries, like France, clearly get more health care for the money put into the system than others. A lack of competition will most likely lead to inefficiency and less innovative solutions. A system based exclusively on tax funding puts a cap on supply, leading to waiting lists for patients and low wages for staff.[142] It can be noticed that Switzerland and the Netherlands, two countries with a very high degree of private health care, get very high scores in the index. Add to this a rising demand due to demographic trends and preferences about how to use the increased income, and there is a growing need for reform.

[141] Health Consumer Powerhouse (2007).

[142] Docteur & Oxley (2003).

More private providers are needed to increase innovation, competition and efficiency in health care provision. It is also essential to create a competitive environment for further research, development and marketing of pharmaceuticals, and in this area intellectual property rights are important. The International Property Rights Index shows that in the US and Northern Europe intellectual property rights are fairly well protected—though not perfectly—and that much needs to be done elsewhere.[143] There is also a need in many countries to open up health care to more private funding, which would increase competition further by creating more choice for patients. It would also increase funding to meet rising demand for health care.

As a result, several countries have carried out health care reforms. These reforms have usually not opened up for private funding—just private provision, tax funded. France, Germany, the UK, the Netherlands and Sweden have opened up for private hospitals and thereby competition in the provision of health care services.[144] Market-oriented reforms have been undertaken without making access more unequal, rather the opposite. Numerous ideas and proposals have been put forth by researchers and in the public debate on possible reforms and management improvements.[145] Some evidence suggests that health savings accounts, introduced in countries like Singapore and the US, empower health care consumers and improve the incentives for cost control.[146] An argument against competition in health care has been the presence of "moral hazard"—that health care consumers will demand "too much" care due to low marginal costs for the insured. There is, however, evidence that this will not happen if insurance

---

[143] IPRI (2007).

[144] OECD (2006b).

[145] In the management field, McKinsey Global Institute (2007) makes a substantial contribution.

[146] Kaplan (2005).

markets are competitive. One study pointed out that "more competition (in health care) is socially beneficial".[147] But reforms have been limited in most countries: only Eastern and Central Europe have seen changes of a more comprehensive nature.[148]

However, health care has improved in several ways, despite a common lack of substantial reform. This is largely a consequence of technological development and new and better pharmaceuticals being developed. Globalisation also offers new ways of introducing more health care supply, competition and cost control. A country like India has emerged as a strong exporter of health care services—either by people coming to another country for treatment or via telecommunication. But to solve remaining problems, meet increasing demands and make health care a dynamic and growing part of society, further reform is needed.

Education

Education is commonly regarded as the primary tool for helping those who have the misfortune of being born under difficult circumstances. By becoming educated and competent, everyone will have fair chances to create a good life. And since increasing productivity per person is what drives growth and incomes, and such a rise is partly driven by more knowledge invested in production, education is central for overall prosperity. Education is one of the welfare services (the other main ones are health care and elderly care) which in most OECD countries is tax-funded and delivered largely by the public sector.

---

[147] Gaynor, Haas-Wilson & Vogt (1998).

[148] Saltman & Figueras, eds (1997).

FIGURE 18. PERCENTAGE OF 15-YEAR-OLD PUPILS USING COMPUTERS, PISA 2003.[151]

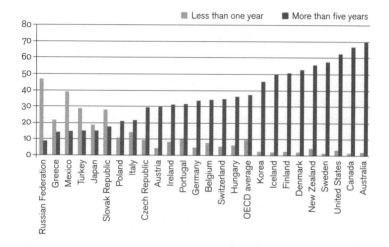

Source: OECD

The so-called PISA study in 2003 compared the average scores in a mathematics test. Taking away the extremes, it is clear that students' average scores in several of the top-performing countries are some 20 per cent higher than the average scores in many of the bottom ones.[149] The variation may not be enormous, but it is there, and there should be room for improvement. Countries that have cut public spending have generally not cut spending on education.[150] Figure 18 might be more illustrative of differences. Societies in general and schools in particular have been very different in quickly adopting the new communications technology, a tool that might quickly improve possibi-

[149] OECD (2007b).

[150] Hauptmeier & Heipertz (2006).

[151] OECD (2007b).

lities for students. Since 2003, when the latest PISA study was conducted—the situation is likely to have changed, with all levels probably rising. But this shows dramatic differences in adaptation of the new technologies by education systems.

In explaining the differences, there is an issue of management, of whether or not to have knowledge as the main priority—something that is generally acknowledged to have contributed to Finland's success. There is also a relevant issue pertaining to the role and authority of teachers. A more structural perspective, where public monopolies again tend to create problems, may also be taken. Countries that have introduced school choice, sometimes through voucher systems, have opened up education to competition and analyses have pointed to improvements in both efficiency and education quality.[152] Indicators also show that immigrant pupils and pupils with special educational needs tend to gain the most from school choice.[153]

Considering the importance of knowledge and research for economic success, it is of course relevant to have high-performing universities. Newsweek has evaluated the world's universities using methods from Shanghai Jiatong University and The Times Higher Education Survey, and the top 20 can be found in Table 3. The Times' ranking system itself reaches very similar conclusions when it comes to the list of the best universities.[154] All the best universities are located in the US and the UK. The highest ranked Continental European university is in Switzerland at number 21. This naturally poses quite a serious problem for Europe.

---

[152] Sandström (2002).

[153] Ahlin (2003).

[154] The Times Higher Education Supplements (2007).

TABLE 4. TOP 20 UNIVERSITIES GLOBALLY 2006[155]

1. Harvard University	9. University of California at San Francisco
2. Stanford University	
3. Yale University	10. Columbia University
4. California Institute of Technology	11. University of Michigan at Ann Arbor
	12. University of California at Los Angeles
5. University of California at Berkeley	13. University of Pennsylvania
	14. Duke University
6. University of Cambridge	15. Princeton University
	16. Tokyo University
7. Massachusetts Institute of Technology	17. Imperial College London
	18. University of Toronto
8. Oxford University	19. Cornell University
	20. University of Chicago

Source: Newsweek

The main common feature among European universities is the political control: universities are part of the public sector. This is reflected in their boards, their funding, their priorities and in their teachings. Frequent reform recommendations therefore include: increase private funding, partly by tuition fees; foster competition; introduce vouchers; decrease state control; and create better incentives for research.[156] Tuition fees are sometimes regarded as controversial, since policymakers fear making access to higher education less equal. But there will always be scholarships and opportunities to take student loans. And the main result of more private funding

---

[155] *Newsweek* (2006).

[156] Bas & van der Ploeg (2005).

would be to add resources that were simply not there before, hence leading to a greater supply of higher education and better quality.

Product and Financial Markets

Imagine regulations demanding that hairdressers have to be closed on Mondays, that there is a limit on the number of tour guides permitted in a city, that petrol stations are forbidden to sell anything but oil products, that you cannot sell your motorbike without a lawyer drafting a complicated contract, and a fixed number of taxi licences are available in cities that does not change through the decades. Until recently, that was the case in Italy.[157] Such regulations will inevitably distort supply and demand, hamper competition and entrepreneurship and make consumer almost powerless. Anyone who has ever tried to hire a taxi in Rome will be familiar with the situation. Regulations like these are common in a number of countries, particularly in Western Europe.

The adverse effects on economic development—productivity, structural change, employment and in the end growth—are well known.[159] Since a number of product markets have been deregulated, there is a lot of evidence about the positive effects. Of course, they may differ, due to differences in reform design and implementation. European telecom markets have largely been deregulated, and since 2000 the EU weighted average charge of a three-minute phone call has fallen by 65 per cent and the cost of a ten-minute call by 74 per cent.[160] Similar developments have been observed in other deregulated product

---

[157] Barber & Michaels (2007).

[159] See, for example, McKinsey Global Institute (2003).

[160] Reding (2006).

FIGURE 19. PRODUCT MARKET REGULATION, OECD COUNTRIES, 1998 AND 2003.[158]

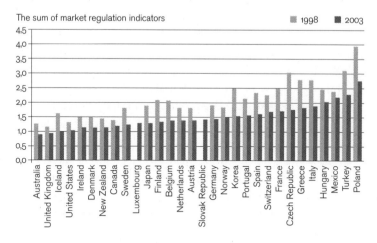

Source: OECD

markets. The evidence suggests that there will be significant positive effects on employment following deregulation in product markets in highly regulated countries.[161] This is why attempts are being made to deregulate these markets, nationally and internationally.

Figure 19 shows the degree of product market regulation in OECD countries in 1998 and 2003, measured as the sum of market regulations in each country and with high numbers indicating a greater degree of regulation. The level of regulation was lower in every OECD country in 2003 compared to 1998. The diagram shows that there are differences, but also that most countries still have a lot to do. The ideal might not be zero regulation since some regulations

---

[158] OECD Statistical Database (2000).

[161] Nicoletti & Scarpetta (2005).

attempt to make the market work better rather than inhibit them. But there are a number of harmful regulations left to tackle for politicians.

Take the financial services industry. The way the financial sector works will affect important aspects of society such as the availability of capital, investment levels and people's savings. During the 1980s, several financial markets, such as capital markets and monetary systems, were reformed. But a large volume of separate national regulations still exist which restrict openness and competition within the financial markets. There is evidence of a positive correlation between financial sector competition and financial openness. The more financial competition there is, the higher a country's economic growth.[162] An increasing globalisation effect is visible in financial services, which leads to more transactions, competition and efficiency—but a lot remains to be done.[163]

Society as a whole loses from the regulation of product, service and financial markets. It is an illusion that even those protected by the regulations benefit. Many attempts to deregulate and liberalise product markets are, however, often met with fierce resistance by those affected and protected by the current, regulated order. There may be strikes and demonstrations. Small, but well organised, special interests protest against changes that would increase conditions for both producers and consumers, especially in the long run. Protected producers resist deregulation that would in particular benefit vastly larger numbers of consumers. This is part of everyday political life and a challenge for a reformer.

---

[162] Francois & Schuknecht (1999).

[163] The historic perspective of this development is well described in Dilip (2006).

Entrepreneurship

Entrepreneurs have been increasingly welcomed by politicians, from left to right. As traditional jobs are rationalised and big corporations tend to hire most people abroad, the hope lies in having more new, expanding businesses. It has become fairly apparent that a society must be dynamic and always renew its production in order to be competitive, and entrepreneurs often come up with the new ideas. There is also a correlation between the ease of doing business and a country's score on the UNDP Human Development Index.[164] This view of entrepreneurs is quite a contrast to a few decades ago, when large-scale production, to which many public institutions, systems and policies were adapted, was the norm in many countries. The old institutions and policies are still largely in place, creating a need for reform.

The Global Entrepreneurship Monitor combines the new business owners with those in the process of starting a business, and thus creates a figure for what it refers to as "early-stage entrepreneurship activity". The highest levels of entrepreneurship are in Australia, the US and the UK, and the lowest levels are in Belgium, Canada and the Czech Republic. As always, there are probably a number of historical explanations for the differences, such as the presence or absence of an entrepreneurship culture. But institutions matter too. People are rational. If the state makes it hard, expensive, bureaucratic and risky to start a business, people are more likely to be deterred. A number of things affect the climate for entrepreneurship. These are whether it is easy or hard to obtain venture capital (which is largely determined by how financial markets work); whether it is easy or

---

[164] World Bank, Doing Business 2005, Removing Obstacles to Growth, World Bank, International Finance Corporation, Oxford University Press, 2005, http://www.doingbusiness.org

FIGURE 20. EARLY-STAGE ENTREPRENEURSHIP ACTIVITY
IN SELECTED OECD COUNTRIES, 2006.[165]

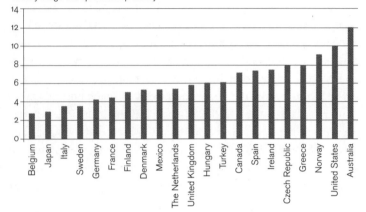

Per cent of the adult population that participate
in early-stage entrepreneurship activity

Source: Global Entrepreneurship Monitor

hard and risky to hire (which is largely determined by the labour market); and whether you are able to retain a small or large part of the money you earn (which is largely determined by tax levels).

An illustrative example of how public systems may affect entrepreneurship is the degree of tax bureaucracy. Figure 21, taken from a study by PriceWaterhouseCoopers and the World Bank, shows how many hours it takes in different countries to comply with the tax code. The higher the number of hours, the more time that entrepreneurs must devote to taxes instead of doing business. The differences are substantial, and this naturally matters for an entrepreneur too, not just the tax rates. One study compared the levels of entrepreneurship in OECD countries with the degree of economic freedom, finding

---

[165] Bosma & Harding (2006).

FIGURE 21. HOURS PER YEAR FOR AN ENTREPRENEUR
TO COMPLY WITH THE TAX CODE IN OECD COUNTRIES, 2006.[166]

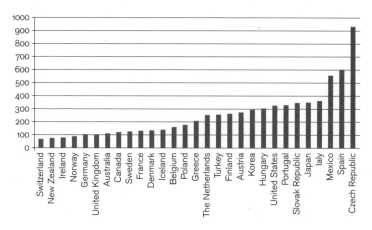

Source: PriceWaterhouseCoopers, World Bank

a strong correlation between low levels of entrepreneurship and a low degree of economic freedom (major state interventions) and vice versa.[167] This is one field where there is a great potential for improvement and thus a need for reform.

Summary and Conclusions

Some countries have top positions in most categories of economic and social success, others have high positions in some categories, and a number of countries have mediocre or low positions throughout. No country can ever be perfect, so there will always be room for improvement. Most countries have a substantial need for reform.

---

[166] The World Bank (2006a).

[167] Björnskov & Foss (2006).

Reforms that liberalise the economy and set off higher growth rates have important social effects. Indeed, many OECD countries, notably in Western Europe, have suffered for a long time from low growth, high unemployment, stagnating living standards and social exclusion. But a number of countries have succeeded well, after launching reforms. That in itself is proof that reforms work and that nations can improve their situation.

Sometimes, institutes and authors introduce new measures for success, which are usually highly interesting and thought-provoking. Robert Putnam wrote about the need for a vibrant civic society in order to gain success.[168] Richard Florida identified talent and tolerance as factors of success.[169] And of course the UNDP has its Human Development Report.[170] These may all contain sympathetic views and they have a point that many traditional measures do not capture all of reality. But they have found it hard to prove robust correlations for their new indicators with actual results in real societies. For example, at least as much would suggest that tolerance comes with increased prosperity as the other way around. These intriguing and inspiring indicators and indexes have generally speaking explained rather little, though they have prompted fruitful discussions. Furthermore, they have limited relevance for the analysis of political reform strategy since the factors are largely far beyond politicians' reach.

The kind of reforms and their direction that are needed to solve problems and improve the situation is well established. New evidence is added to that knowledge day by day. This does not mean that every country should do exactly the same as everyone else, but rather that

---

[168] Putnam (2000).

[169] Florida (2002).

[170] UNDP (2006).

reforms must be adapted to national conditions. Obviously, the first aim for any country must be to avoid counter-reforms that actually worsen the situation and are motivated by populist, symbolic or other short-sighted reasons. This includes avoiding protectionism, higher taxes, increased market regulation, a tighter political grip on higher education, more bureaucracy, limits to trade or to competition in welfare services and social security, more benefits for not working, and growth in public expenditure. Choosing not to act when faced with today's problems or rising challenges is also an active choice.

Quite a few reforms are needed. In the shorter run, lower taxes on work, deregulation in the labour market, competition in the provision of health care, school choice, a more flexible retirement age, more restrictive social security systems, more openness to trade, and deregulation for entrepreneurs would be important steps. In the longer perspective, reforms are about continuing to increase econo-mic freedom by opening up social security and welfare services for private funding, opening up for mobility in general, freeing up and improving the education system, defusing the demographic challenge, reducing tax pressures and changing welfare systems to be enabling rather than creating dependency, and in general creating a society that embraces change in order to provide better living standards and social conditions. Every country has done something and quite a number of countries have come far—though even more remains to be done.

COUNTRIES THAT HAVE ACHIEVED A LOT

"The state today needs to be enabling and based on a partnership with the citizen, one of mutual rights and responsibilities. The implications are profound. Public services need to go through the same revolution—professionally, culturally and in organisation—that the private sector has been through."

TONY BLAIR, FORMER UK PRIME MINISTER[171]

"To achieve change and reform you need to have political power, a vision, strong will and courage."

IVAN MIKLOS, FORMER FINANCE MINISTER OF SLOVAKIA[172]

"Consensus for quality decisions does not arise before they are made and implemented. It develops progressively after they are taken, as they deliver satisfactory outcomes to the public... Do not try to advance a step at a time. Define your objectives clearly and move towards them by quantum leaps. Otherwise the interest groups will have time to mobilise and drag you down... Let the dog see the rabbit. People cannot co-operate with the reform process unless they know where you are heading."

ROGER DOUGLAS,
FORMER NEW ZEALAND FINANCE MINISTER[173]

A NUMBER OF OECD COUNTRIES have managed to launch substantial reforms. They have solved serious problems and turned the status quo around. New ideas were adopted, policy proposals were

---

[171] Blair (2007).
[172] Miklos (2007).
[173] Douglas (1998).

shaped, a reform agenda was defended, decisions were made and reforms were implemented. And the results have often far exceeded expectations. This is the fascinating story of leadership, change, ideas and success. The reformist countries have managed to carry out far-reaching reforms—sometimes a few, sometimes many and partly in different areas of society. What they did and how they did it provides sources of advice and inspiration for others.

In any research that has to do with society, there will always be uncertainty about what actually is creating the effects. Thus, there are always many attempts to claim that negative results are not the result of poor policies and positive results not necessarily the results of good policies. Those responsible for problems which stem from bad policies will always try to say that the causes of the problems are beyond their reach. Similarly, they will try to deny the success of others or point out that the success is due to something other than the policies. It is important to try to establish what is true and not. One way to do this can be to travel to different countries.

Added together, the separate countries show that outcomes are largely the effect of policies and that such policies can be introduced with positive effects regardless of geography, size, religion and degree of problems. A closer look at individual countries not only shows that things have happened in several places and that reform is possible; it also reveals parts of how those reforms may be achieved. Here, therefore, we present separate stories of countries that did a lot, focusing on reforms that have been thought of as impossible or at least very hard to launch. These are also the stories of the people—politicians, advisors, economists and civil servants—who did it. The stories are told without any special order as to which countries or reforms have been the most successful.[174]

The Celtic Tiger

On the more romantic side, the Republic of Ireland is traditionally known for being green, for fairytales, Guinness, friendliness and great writers. The grimmer traditional image is that of a rainy, poor and religiously controlled society plagued by conflicts. Yet a visitor to modern Dublin is struck by the sight of new roads, shining new office buildings, rows of nice shops, much of it combined with tradition. The grimness is far away. Ireland was once the poorest country in Western Europe, from which a quarter of the population emigrated. There are now almost ten times more people of Irish descent living abroad than there are actual inhabitants of Ireland.[175]

Today's Ireland is a very different country from the historic image. It has had net immigration for more than a decade. Since the European Union's enlargement in 2004, hundreds of thousands of Poles, Czechs and other East and Central European citizens have come to Ireland to work. Its population is now 4.1 million and it is the second wealthiest country in Western Europe, surpassed only by Luxembourg. Today, more people probably associate Ireland with U2 than with a strict Catholic Church.

The 26 southern counties that comprise today's Republic of Ireland gained their independence from Britain in 1921. In 1948, Ireland withdrew from the British Commonwealth and it entered the European Community in 1973. In 1999, Ireland was among the first 11 EU countries to introduce the euro. Ireland had some reasonably good years in the 1960s, but by 1980 the country had developed serious economic problems. In the words of The Economist, "Fifteen years

---

[174] Many parts of the country information come from the CIA (2007).

[175] Hellman & Rankka (1999).

ago Ireland was deemed an economic failure, a country that after years of mismanagement was suffering from an awful cocktail of high unemployment, slow growth, high inflation, heavy taxation and towering public debts." In 1988, The Economist referred to Ireland as "poorest of the rich" but by 1997 it was "Europe's shining light".[176]

Another decade later, in 2007, one can conclude that this light has continued to burn just as brightly. GDP per capita is today almost 40 per cent above the European Union average—in 1987 it was 31 per cent below that average. In that context, it matters little that at least a few per cent of the Irish GDP is profits earned by foreign companies in Ireland and repatriated abroad. Average personal income increased by 102 per cent between 1994 and 2003, and incomes for the 10 per cent of the population with the lowest incomes increased by 59 per cent. The share of households with low income (below $20,000 in disposable income a year) dropped from 43 per cent in 1990 to 14 per cent in 2004.[177]

The turning point was in 1987. Public debt was more than 100 per cent of GDP and Ireland's credit rating was low. In the early 1980s, taxes had been raised and in 1987, taxes on an average income amounted to some 60 per cent. Emigration had reached new heights and a common joke at the time was "Will the last Irishman to leave please turn out the lights?". In 1987, the government launched a "Programme for National Recovery". It was intended to be the only one but was followed by three similar reform packages. The main initial aim was to cut public expenditure and achieve fiscal consolidation. This effort was successful. In 1987, public expenditure was 52 per cent of GDP and in 2005 it was 35 per cent.[178] This may look like

---

[176] *The Economist* (2004c).

[177] Euromonitor International (2006).

a radical cut, but in fact the public sector has much more money now than in the 1980s, thanks to the economy now being several times larger.

Politicians like Charles Haughey, Garret Fitzgerald and Ray Mac-Sharry—the latter for a while nicknamed Mac the Knife for his cuts in public expenditure—were important people in this process.[179] The work of the National Economic and Social Council and its experts has been described as important in innovating, shaping and promoting the reform policies. A special working group of business leaders, trade union leaders and civil servants was also instrumental in drawing up the competitiveness reforms. The group is said to have been inspired by "The Competitiveness of Nations", a book by Michael Porter.[180] In the Irish corporatist tradition, there were also other committees and groups with similar tasks.

Ireland also reduced the corporate tax levels stepwise, from 50 per cent in 1985 all the way to the 12.5 per cent of today. Corporate tax revenues increased from about 1 per cent of GDP to 4 per cent of GDP during that period.[181] This follows the so-called Laffer Curve, where lower taxes unleash more economic activity and tax revenues actually increase. It should, however, also be remembered that the amount of money left in the private sector, in the hands of people and corporations, increased even faster than tax revenue. In the Irish case, the lower corporate tax rates helped bring a sharp increase in foreign direct investment. Ireland receives about one quarter of US foreign direct investment in Europe and now has about 1,100 multinational companies on its soil.

---

[178] OECD Economic Outlook, 2005

[179] *The Economist* (2004c), Hellman & Rankka (1999).

[180] Government of Sweden (1999).

[181] Mitchell (2004).

During the 1990s, successive governments also made some cuts in the personal income tax rate, with the lowest level being cut from 35 per cent to 26 per cent and the highest from 58 to 46 per cent. Ireland has also benefited from a substantial labour supply, first due to its relatively young population and second due to immigration. The number of people in work rose by 50 per cent between 1993 and 2003. Studies also point to the Irish workforce being well educated and there was an early supply of engineers, business school graduates and scientists when demand for their services started rising.[182]

It is sometimes claimed that the European Union is the main explanation of Ireland's economic success. Certainly, being part of the Single Market has most likely had a positive impact, as access to a larger market is important to all small economies. But what this point often refers to is that Ireland has also received substantial contributions from the EU Structural Funds, which allegedly explains the economic boom. The Irish Economic and Social Research Institute has studied this and concluded that EU funds may explain 10 per cent of the GDP increase in the 1990s.[183] Other studies have pointed to the funds adding about 0.5 per cent to GDP growth a year, which is not irrelevant but hardly crucial considering that growth has been 6–7 per cent a year for 15 years.[184] Though limited, the EU Structural Funds have probably had a positive impact, possibly on strengthening several Irish institutions, and have been one small part of a very positive circle of improvement.[185]

The Irish political landscape, like that of any country, has its own peculiarities. The two biggest parties, Fianna Fáil and Fine Gael, have

---

[182] *The Economist* (2004c).

[183] Honohan, ed (1997).

[184] *The Economist* (2004c).

[185] Özenen (2006).

been more divided by history, culture, image and supporters than by actual differences in policy. In policy, they are fairly pragmatic and have both contributed in different ways to the reform process. The 1987 reform package was a product of a coalition between Fine Gael and Labour, Ireland's third biggest political party. Ireland is currently governed by Fianna Fáil and the Progressive Democrats.

Several common explanations for the reforms include a general insight among people that there was a need for change, and the fact that the major political parties agreed on the need for reform. Reforms were possible to launch in co-operation with the trade union movement, partly because the latter feared that witholding their consent might prompt a development similar to that in Margaret Thatcher's Britain, where many reforms were enacted to limit trade union power.[186] The Irish also focused on reforms that were likely to have a quick result, such as cutting corporate taxes. Quick results may increase the support for further reforms and make it easier to initiate reforms in the first place.

For all its success, Ireland still has problems and faces new challenges that can be met with further reform. The EU now has a number of new member states attracting foreign direct investment with low taxes. Two possible issues of concern in the medium term include the fiscal development and Ireland's rapidly rising property prices. The OECD recommends strengthening work incentives for women and lone parents and improving access to education.[187] It has also pointed to a number of areas of Irish society where there is a need for increased competition through deregulation: retail trade, pharmacies, legal and

---

[186] Hellman & Rankka (1999).
[187] OECD (2007a).

medical services, electricity, telecommunications and inter-city buses.[187]

The Quiet Boom

A vast and remote place, Australia seemed to the British during the time of the Empire like a suitable place for a self-sustaining prison. Today, it is not only one of the world's wealthiest countries but also a place where many people choose to go voluntarily and is very open to immigrants. Its population stands at 20.5 million. Australia may be well known for things like the Great Barrier Reef, the Sydney Opera House and kangaroos—but the best-loved person in Australian folklore is the "battler", someone with a fighting spirit. It is this quality that the country has exhibited in turning around its economic development.

In 1901, when Australia became an independent federation, it was actually the wealthiest country in the world (of course facing much less limited global competition and with a different level of prosperity compared to today). By 1950, it was in eighth place in the global GDP per capita rankings but by 1990 had slipped to 18th, testifying to a steady decline (though with reasonable growth rates at times, such as in the 1960s). Australia experienced two major recessions in the early 1980s and early 1990s, when both GDP and employment decreased.[189] But it has now regained its position and its GDP per capita is back at number 8 in a world of tougher competition than ever before.

---

[188] Rae, Vogt & Wise (2006).
[189] *The Economist* (2005b).

"Two hundred years after Captain Philip and the First Fleet arrived in Sydney Cove, Australians were accustomed to drought, flood and fire, to booms and busts… They had experienced every circumstance except the one economic circumstance they most wanted and least expected: a very long period where everything simply got better and better. Then in the middle of 1991, unheralded and unnoticed, Australia began what would prove to be the longest boom in its history."[190]

Thus wrote John Edwards, HSBC Bank chief economist for Australia and New Zealand and former senior economic adviser to national treasurer and then prime minister Paul Keating. Australia has now had 16 consecutive years of growth, inflation has remained fairly low and unemployment is the lowest for 30 years. Per capita real income per person has increased by 40 per cent during this period and per capita wealth has risen by twice as much. The 20 per cent with the lowest incomes have experienced the highest income rise of all groups.[191]

The main causes of this "quiet economic boom" can be found in the reforms of mainly the 1980s and the 1990s and the country's subsequent increased integration in the global economy. The most important early reforms included: deregulated financial markets; virtual elimination of what had been rather high tariffs; introduction of a floating exchange rate; and labour market reforms that increased efficiency, partly by transferring wage bargaining from industry level towards enterprise level. Companies were privatised and a number of product markets were deregulated and competition thereby increased. The role of the state gradually changed from interventionist to setting the regulatory framework for the market. Corporate

---

[190] Edwards (2006).

[191] Edwards (2006).

tax rates were cut, first from 49 per cent to 39 per cent and then to 33 per cent in just five years. A number of measures were also taken to achieve a federal regulatory standard, in 1995 consolidated with the National Competition Policy of 1995.

The reforms focused largely on numerous changes at the micro level[192] and were initiated and implemented by Labour governments. Paul Keating was a key figure in the process. In the 1980s, he said that Australia was becoming a banana republic and was re-elected after the first wave of rather radical reforms. The Liberal party supported the reforms when in opposition and since entering government has kept the budget under tight control, thereby reducing public debt to a record low. The Liberals have also launched new reforms, such as making the central bank independent. John Howard has now been prime minister for ten years. His leadership has often been praised, one journalist noting that Howard "implements unpopular policies and makes them popular".[193]

Australia is very open and integrated in the world economy. It has, for example, a rare bilateral trade agreement with the US. Exports are now almost four times higher in value than in 1991 and exports as a share of GDP have risen from about 10 per cent in the mid-1980s to about 20 per cent of GDP today. Terms of trade—how much a country actually gets paid for its exports—have improved for the past ten years. Immigration has been embraced and the official government website has a "Choose Australia" title on its migration page.[194]

---

[192] A detailed yet accessible account of the reforms in Australia are compiled by the Commonwealth of Australia, Industry Commission (1998).

[193] Crosby (2006).

[194] Government of Australia, website.

Australian reforms took place before, between and after the two periods of recession. A crisis might open the window of reform a bit more, but would not be decisive. The crises in Australia took place at similar times as crises for other wealthy nations and partly for the same reasons, such as international shocks and the short-term transformative consequences of bringing high inflation down and reducing state intervention in the economy. Evidence suggests that Australians tend to support reforms not out of ideology but by seeing concrete positive effects.[195] By launching these reforms, Australian governments have finally achieved their aim of a long period of sustained growth and improved living standards.

Some problems do remain, however, and the world poses new economic and social challenges. One problem for Australia is its rather low employment rate for low-productivity workers, which demands further reform of labour market and social insurance systems.[196] Efforts to shift more people from welfare into work are desirable. Reforms that have been identified as relevant for the future include: changes to disability benefit schemes; improvements of upper-secondary school attainments; strengthening competition in network industries; further tax cuts; and and a more flexible labour market.[197]

The New Europe

A reason why Donald Rumsfeld's snap about certain parts of Western Europe being "old"—indirectly implying that other parts represented the new—created such a stir was probably that he just put words on

---

[195] Norton (2005).

[196] Frijtres & Gregory (2006).

[197] OECD (2007a), *The Economist* (2005b)

the thoughts of many. During the turbulent years when the Berlin Wall came down and the Iron Curtain was lifted, there were many worries and fears for the future. A general belief was that the countries in the East would never be able to compete with the West and would most likely be dependent on foreign aid for decades. There was also a debate about whether they should choose stepwise reforms or "shock therapy" to get away from the disaster of the centrally planned economy. Today, we can see the astonishing results. Most countries in Eastern and Central Europe have developed better than anyone dared to hope, due to free-market reforms, and the countries that have fared best were the ones that launched the most radical reforms.[198] This has, in turn, enhanced competition and reform throughout Europe. In 2003, the year before the eastward enlargement, 36 reforms to facilitate doing business were carried out in European countries out of 89 globally, and eight of the top ten reformers were European.[199]

Foreign direct investment in Eastern and Central Europe has boomed, with EU companies investing about 150 billion in these countries since the early 1990s. Exports increased strongly following liberalisation of foreign trade. Hungary's exports rose, for example, by 380 per cent and Czech exports rose by 280 per cent in the ten years before EU entry.[200] Incomes have risen and poverty rates have fallen. The high growth rates of Eastern and Central Europe have also contributed to higher growth rates in Western Europe. The ten new EU countries from Eastern and Central Europe, with some 100 million inhabitants, still account for only about 7 per cent of EU

---

[198] An extensive account of this process is to be found in Åslund (2007a).

[199] World Bank, Doing Business 2005, Removing Obstacles to Growth, World Bank, International Finance Corporation, Oxford University Press, 2005, http://www.doingbusiness.org

[200] Barysch (2006).

GDP—the EU has had 492 million inhabitants in January 2007—but the share is growing.[201]

It is sometimes claimed that most of this growth is just about catching up with the wealthiest countries and that when these countries do so, their growth will fade. It is probably partly true that they are catching up, helped to a great extent by the availability of imported technology and skills. But the evidence suggests that catching up is just a small part of the explanation. If catching up by poor countries was an automatic mechanism, why did it happen now in Eastern and Central Europe and not in the 1970s or 1980s? A country like Ireland was said to be just catching up, only for it to then surpass most other nations in the prosperity stakes. It is more a matter of growth-friendly institutions and policies, such as openness to trade, low and flat taxes, deregulated markets, improved macroeconomic frameworks, low inflation and limited public expenditure.[202]

The starting-point for these countries in the early 1990s was very different from the situation in most other OECD countries today. They were poor and the old system was obviously totally incapable of delivering anything but problems. Still, there are reasons to take a look at these countries in a reform perspective today. First, it is important to see which policies actually work and what direction reforms should take. Second, there are strategic lessons: despite the great problems 15 years ago there were obstacles to reform, uncertainty about its direction and speed and it was hard to know where to begin. Third, a main cause of economic problems, especially in Western Europe, has been excessive state intervention in the economy and the problems in Eastern and Central Europe had a similar

---

[201] European Central Bank (2007).

[202] Åslund (2007a).

root, though different in extent. Ivan Miklos, former finance minister of Slovakia, thinks there is much for the West to learn. "The areas that need reform, such as social security systems, labour markets, welfare services, are largely the same and the reasons for the problems are similar."[203]

Every country in Eastern and Central Europe has an intriguing story to tell, and it has been told eloquently and extensively elsewhere.[204] Two—Estonia and Slovakia—can illustrate the success and may be of particular use when analysing reform strategies. Estonia today has a population of 1.3 million. I visited the Estonian capital Tallinn in 2007, 14 years since my last visit, and found the difference dramatic. In 1993, two years after the liberation from the Soviet Union and communism, the old Hanseatic city of Tallinn was deeply depressing. Houses were falling apart, the streets were dirty, there were hardly any restaurants and people seemed genuinely miserable. Army hats from the Soviet Union and vodka were two of only a few products sold on the street corners. Tallinn today is simply shining. There are many new office buildings, the old town has been renovated, restaurants abound, people communicate a sense of well-being, technology seems to be present everywhere and there is activity wherever you look. Of course, some parts of the city still retain traces of the old, but what has happened is nothing short of remarkable.

Tallinn shows what happens if a country launches radical free-market reforms. In 2006, growth in Estonia exceeded 11 per cent.[205] Average income has risen by 120 per cent in the last ten years. Incomes for the 10 per cent with the lowest incomes have risen by 160 per cent.[206] The

---

[203] Miklos (2007).

[204] See Zsiga (forthcoming).

[205] Eurostat (1996).

[206] Euromonitor International (2006).

Estonian Environment Information Centre shows that the environment has improved in many ways in Estonia, again stressing the need to grow economically to get greener.[207] According to the World Database of Happiness, Estonians are also much happier today, which is also apparent in most other reformist countries for which there are sufficient time-series.[208] Estonia is now a member of the EU and Nato.

Under the leadership of Mart Laar, Estonia swiftly abandoned the collapsing centrally planned economy. Instead, the recipe was privatisation, deregulation, tax cuts and e-government. In 1994, Estonia introduced a flat tax of 26 per cent tax for everyone regardless of income. Laar was warned that a flat tax would be impossible. It was not. Tax revenues have increased every year since 1994, despite reductions in the tax rate to 22 per cent (soon to be 18 per cent). The current government's stated aim is a 12 per cent flat tax. Estonia actually initiated the flat tax trend.

Many of Estonia's reformers were not politicians initially. Laar, for instance, was a history professor. But since the established politicians were part of the old system, there had to be new people coming in. A main question at the time was of course if they should emulate the economic and social policies and systems of Western Europe, but they chose not to because they wanted to achieve different results. However, they did get many of their ideas from Western think-tanks and institutes. The political leaders were not experts in economic theory or policy, but they knew the broad picture.

---

[207] Estonian Information Centre (2007).
[208] World Database of Happiness, website.

The reformers faced resistance from special interests, and in countries that had experienced a large amount of propaganda about the dangers of the market and the decadence of the West, there were fears and counter-reactions at first. But there was decisive political action and the opponents were confronted. The abolition of all tariffs on foreign trade by Estonia—the first country after World War II to do so unilaterally—is also an interesting case of reform strategy. The Estonians believed they had to abolish all tariffs, without exception, since that would always have provided other industries with an argument to have tariffs for "protection", creating a slippery slope towards more trade restrictions.[209]

Going a bit further to the south, then, what are the reform lessons from Slovakia? In 1993, Czechoslovakia was peacefully dissolved (it had existed since World War I after the dissolution of the Austro-Hungarian Empire) and the Slovak Republic was founded, with a population of 5.5 million. For most of the 1990s, Slovakia did not reform like other countries in the region and its political leadership under Vladimir Meciar was authoritarian and populist. Slovakia's prospects looked bleak and it seemed unlikely that the country would be able to join the EU in the foreseeable future.

In 1998, a new government was elected. It proceeded to launch a series of reforms, including flat income tax of 19 per cent, privatisation, deregulation, macroeconomic stabilisation and increased openness. Economic growth became one of the highest in Europe at 5–8 per cent annually and unemployment dropped from 19 per cent in 2000 to 13.6 per cent in 2006, thus remaining quite high.[210] In 2004, Slovakia was among the group of ten new EU entrants, having

---

[209] Erixon (forthcoming).

[210] Eurostat (1996).

enacted substantial reforms to meet the entry criteria. Following the economic reforms, Slovakia managed to attract considerable volumes of foreign direct investment. Indeed, the country has become the world's largest car producer relative to its size. A visitor to the capital Bratislava these days will still find that the communist regime's highway cuts brutally through the Old Town, but they will also see many signs of progress.

The reformist government was re-elected once, but in the election of 2006, the opposition formed a new coalition government. The government is led by Robert Fico of Smer, the party of Vladimir Meciar returned and there are a few xenophobic forces involved. In the election campaign, Fico promised to roll back reforms, not least the flat tax, in order to end the Slovakian "gold rush", which was odd given how much Slovakians had benefited from the investments.[211] This was widely reported as evidence that reform was unpopular and that reformers tend to lose elections. However, the main party of the previous government, and indeed the most reformist one, gained votes in the 2006 election. It was the lack of support for some smaller parties and their tactical moves that in the end paved the way for a new government. Contrary to some reports, therefore, democratic support for the Slovak reformers actually rose in 2006.

Since the 2006 election none of the main reforms, including the flat tax, has been rolled back, as promised. True, the new government is not pressing ahead with further reform, but neither is it undoing what has been done. This is an important lesson, also confirmed by similar developments in many other reformist countries. Reforms are usually not repealed, simply because although they may be unpopular at first, nobody wants to go back afterwards. The next election

---

[211] *The Economist* (2006c).

outcome remains to be seen, but it is a fact that it is the previous governments' efforts that pulled Slovakia out of misery to success, and that is already part of the history books.

One lesson from Eastern and Central Europe has been that radical reforms do not always produce immediate positive results. There will be a period of transformation which also poses difficulties. The results will come—and will be more positive if the reforms were more radical—but it takes political persistence.[212] Voters do not necessarily prefer far-reaching changes in these countries either and the political situation in Eastern and Central Europe has been somewhat problematic in the last few years. Important further reforms have stalled.[213] Still, the success of many countries in Eastern and Central Europe is enormous when their situation today is compared with the reality 15 years ago.

An international comparison with other wealthy countries is favourable for these countries in many respects, but it is also apparent that they need to do more. There have been a number of reforms of macroeconomic frameworks, product markets, state-owned companies, taxes and trade. But as in Western Europe, a great deal remains to be done with regard to welfare services, social security and (for countries like Poland) labour markets. Long-term trends such as globalisation will of course have an impact and demographics pose a bigger challenge for many countries in Eastern and Central Europe than for others.[214]

---

[212] More on this topic in Wykoff (2001).

[213] *The Economist* (2007g).

[214] EBRD (2007).

The Rolling Rock

Iceland's landscape is wild and beautiful: volcanoes, treeless expanses, geysers and wild horses. It gets your imagination running towards fictional stories like "The Lord of the Rings". Any visitor is probably struck by an impression of harshness. The first idea that comes to mind is not that it is a natural paradise for people to inhabit. In fact, Iceland has practically no natural resources on land, except geothermal power. But a visitor in recent years might also notice all the modern cars, fashionable shops and rather high prices. Iceland may be a rock in the sea but the rock is really rolling. Since the early 1990s, a series of reforms has made Iceland the fifth wealthiest country in the world. The formerly isolated Danish colony, which once did not receive information of the Danish king's death until months later, is now a centre of commerce, finance, growth and employment.

Iceland has only 300,000 inhabitants. Some people joke that it shouldn't be hard to support such a small number of citizens. Indeed, unemployment is 1.3 per cent today. But the fact is that Iceland had great trouble supporting an even smaller population during much of its history. In the late 19th century, 20 per cent of the population emigrated to the United States, mainly in order to escape famine. And really, why should it be any easier to employ 80 or 90 per cent of a population of 300,000 than 80 or 90 per cent of a population of 300 million? Is the share of successful employers by nature larger in smaller countries? Of course not, and the fact remains that some other small countries do not succeed as well as for example the United States in terms of employment. In 1904, Iceland was granted home rule and in 1944 gained full independence from Denmark. The legislative assembly, the Althing, is the oldest in the world, dating back to the year 930.

Historically, the main part of the economy was based on fishing. In recent decades, aluminium, tourism, software production, banking and biotechnology have emerged and come to represent significant economic sectors. For much of the period after World War II, Iceland experienced a reasonable increase in prosperity, but in the 1980s problems began to mount. Inflation was in the double digits, rising in some months to about 100 per cent on an annual basis and eroding the savings of ordinary people. Public deficits and debt soared. The all-important fishing industry was suffering from overfishing, threatening its future. The Icelandic state was intensely interventionist, for example running fish meal processing plants, a travel agency, a knitting workshop and a printing company. Through state ownership of the commercial banks, financial competition and incentives were limited and the political grip on any Icelandic business was tight.

But the direction of the development was turned 180 degrees by a series of reforms. Professor Hannes H Gissurarsson of the University of Iceland, a close policy advisor to the prime minister at the time, has summarised the main parts of the reforms as cutting subsidies, stabilising the economy, liberalising markets, privatisation, cutting taxes, assigning property rights to natural resources and strengthening pension funds. Inflation came down from 60–70 per cent by the mid-1980s to below 5 per cent by 1992. Public deficits at 4–5 per cent of GDP became surpluses by 1998. Unemployment dropped below 2 per cent. State-owned companies—the travel agency and others—were privatised. More importantly, the banks were also sold to private interests.

Studies have confirmed that liberalisation of product and financial markets alike have been successful.[215] The turnover of the Icelandic

---

[215] Tulip (2007); Lauback & Wise (2005).

banks was seven times higher in 2006 compared to 2002 and 50 per cent of income came from abroad. The corporate tax rate was cut from 45 per cent to 18 per cent and yet corporate tax revenue in 2006 was ten times higher than it was in 1991. Personal income taxes have also been cut substantially, as have payroll taxes. Total government revenue as a share of GDP was 32 per cent in 2006.[216] As a parenthesis, Iceland might provide interesting evidence of the effects of tax cuts on labour supply. Tax reforms made incomes earned in 1987 tax-free, which increased the labour supply by 6.7 per cent that year, mostly among women.[217]

Since overfishing was a consequence of free access to the sea, property rights by quotas were introduced and overfishing is no longer a problem. Furthermore, the fishing industry became more efficient, turning losses into profits by the early 1990s. Average purchasing power increased by almost 5 per cent annually in 1995–2004, strong increases also being noted for people on the lowest incomes. Thus, Icelandic income distribution is still one of the most equal in the OECD. A pension reform in 1998 involved a shift from pay-as-you-go systems to accumulated funds with voluntary private pensions as supplement.[218]

How was all of this possible? David Oddsson, prime minister from 1992 to 2004, points to two decisive underlying factors: *"First, there was the will of the people themselves to normalise their economy. The whole nation suffered because of economic instability, and the ordinary wage-earner was worst hit of all... A second important factor was that the coalition government which was formed in 1991 was based on very*

---

[216] Gissurarsson (2007).

[217] Bianchi, Gudmundsson & Zoega (2000).

[218] Gissurarsson (2007).

clear policies… Politicians who lack clear political vision tend to go astray when there are many complex questions to ponder."

He also points out the need to proceed step by step and to initiate reforms that produce positive results: *"There is little point in hoisting all the sails only to run aground on the nearest rock. But gradually the public noticed that the doomsday prophecies did not come true—far from it, service improved and expanded after privatisation. And support has steadily been growing for the view that market forces need to have as much say as possible."* Oddsson furthermore underlines the importance of responsible trade unions and employers and central bank independence to create a reliable economic framework.

Pointing to the future, Oddsson stresses that globalisation is an opportunity and underlines the need for investments in education, not least in more private universities.[219] Professor Gissurarsson points to the need for further cuts in income and corporate taxes as well as VAT and suggests cuts in import charges and privatisations. Based on indicators, the OECD recommends: reductions in agriculture support, improved upper-secondary education attainment and lower barriers to entry for domestic and foreign firms. Iceland is on the right path but the world is changing and there will always be new demands from new steps in the development. That, in turn, demands further reform.

Probably the Best Labour Policy In the World?

Denmark is a nation of islands, the southernmost part of the Nordic group of five countries, with a population of 5.5 million. It conveys

---

[219] Oddsson (2004).

images of design, Carlsberg, police thrillers and windmills. It has also been a reformist country in various waves during the 1980s and 1990s. The 1980s brought a tax reform, deregulation and some privatisation, only for unemployment to mount in the early 1990s. At that time, Danish society had about one third of the population of working age not working, instead being supported by the state.[220] Starting in 1993, the Danish government launched a number of reforms, including tax cuts, scaled back social benefits and increased limits on benefit periods. Later, the labour market was deregulated, particularly in respect of hiring and firing regulations, income and corporate taxes were cut and wealth tax was abolished. The retirement age has been raised and welfare reforms have been carried out. As growth rates picked up, so did employment. Reforms have occurred during Social Democrat and centre-right administrations alike, with the two most recent prime ministers, Poul Nyrup Rasmussen and Anders Fogh Rasmussen, both being proponents of reform.

Today, Denmark has a positive record on several scores, especially regarding the labour market. On my last visit to Copenhagen, in 2006, I was struck by all the signs saying "Now Hiring!" At about 7 per cent, Denmark has one of the EU's lowest unemployment rates, particularly among young people.[221] One fifth of the Danes lose their jobs every year, and just as many get new jobs.[222] The increase in employment during the last decade has been quite remarkable. Income distribution is still one of the most equal in the OECD. Danish "flexicurity" has been a buzzword for years and is frequently seen as the reason for the success of the country's labour market policies. The impression is that the flexicurity model offers both flexibility and generous public social security, with good results. It is certainly

---

[220] Government of Sweden (1999).

[221] Eurostat (1996).

[222] *The Economist* (2007i).

very much worth a close look, though it is important to analyse openly which parts of the Danish reforms that are behind the strength of the labour market success. Is it really down to flexicurity or to other reforms too?

Put briefly, flexicurity has three pillars: a flexible labour market, generous unemployment benefits and an active labour market policy. Which of these create labour market success? Some countries have a free labour market and less generous public unemployment benefits yet still perform well in employment. But there are no countries with a highly regulated labour market and generous unemployment benefits that are very successful. Hence, the main likely factor behind employment success is flexibility. The rise in the labour supply, measured as annual hours worked, also correlates well with the decrease in the marginal income tax rate from 59 per cent in 1996 to 52 per cent in 2005.[223] That adds a factor usually not seen as part of flexicurity. Several studies have also found evidence that the policies to make unemployed people more active rather than just receive benefits contribute positively to employment.[224] Denmark also has some of the highest scores in the world in terms of its degree of globalisation and protection for property rights, which are also likely to explain parts some of the country's positive development.

The Danish labour market thus changed in many ways with these reforms. It had always retained a high degree of flexibility in hiring and firing but the once highly centralised wage bargaining process became more decentralised and even individualised. Some 80 per cent of Danes belong to a trade union and the unions supported many of the labour market reforms. A number of reforms were also

---

[223] Ågerup (2007).
[224] OECD (2007a).

launched that put limits on unemployment benefits, including a then-controversial limit on how long such benefits can be received, which has been important for reducing unemployment in general and long-term unemployment in particular. The reforms also placed demands on people who were able to work to actually do so, especially the young, since there was a fear of massive long-term unemployment among young people. Marginal taxes were cut to make work more profitable. Initially, it was very controversial to question whether the unemployed actually needed stronger incentives to work, but after the reforms, the Danish labour ministry conducted a survey which showed that the attitudes had become very clear: people now regarded work as the norm.[225]

Denmark's still very high tax pressure, which is partly explained by its high state unemployment benefits, does produce adverse effects (such as low disposable incomes, especially for low-income earners). In Denmark, a quarter of people of working age are still outside the labour force and largely living off the state. Thus, unemployment is down but many jobless people are hidden in large, tax-funded public programmes.[226] This group of socially excluded people has increased from 600,000 to 1,200,000 in the last 25 years.[227] There is thus a need to reduce tax pressure and shift more people from welfare into work. This could still be combined with high unemployment benefits, if they are private rather than publicly funded. If the Danish state were to reduce these public benefits and taxes, there would be more money left in people's hands to save, invest or buy private income insurance as social protection. Another way to achieve a similar result would be to allow people to opt out of the public insurance system by tax deductions.

---

[225] Government of Sweden (1999).

[226] Lang (2006).

[227] Velfærdskommissionen (2005).

The Danish labour market has been producing very positive results, but these are due to the whole package of reforms and not merely the flexicurity reforms—some of which may not even benefit employment. The current Danish government is continuing to cut income and corporate taxes. However, the OECD forecasts the Danish economy to have the slowest growth in the entire OECD area in 2008–2012.[228] This underlines the need for further reform, not least since the successful employment trend has coincided with higher growth rates. For growth to pick up, more people have to start working; for growth to reach 2 per cent annually, 125,000 more people have to be employed.[229] A more successful integration of immigrants into the labour market would be a valuable component of this. The OECD has recommended further cuts in marginal tax rates, privatisation, introduction of competition in welfare services, reform of housing policies and reforms to increase efficiency in the education system.[230]

Making Immigration Work

For decades one of the poorer countries in Western Europe, Spain is today a lot more than sunny beaches, low prices, sangria and bull-fighting. It managed first in the late 1970s to make a peaceful transition from the Franco dictatorship and in the 1980s to become an EU member. It has also reformed its economy substantially, with very positive results. Just ten years ago, GDP per capita was 89.4 per cent of the EU average. In 2007, it is estimated to be 101 per cent of the average—higher, for the first time ever.[231] In fact, Spain's 40.5 million inhabitants are 75 per cent wealthier today than they were 30 years

---

[228] OECD.

[229] Ågerup (2007).

[230] OECD (2007).

[231] Eurostat (1996).

ago, roughly the time when John Cleese as Basil Fawlty in "Fawlty Towers" used to excuse the clumsiness of his employee Manuel with the fact that he was from Barcelona.[232] About one third of all the jobs created in the entire euro-zone since 1992 have been created in Spain.[233] Though plagued by Basque terrorism, Spain is today very successful—stylish and fashionable, not least with Zara opening new shops in city after city throughout Europe. In the words of *The Economist*: "Perhaps no other European country has achieved so much, on so many fronts, so quickly."[234]

Between 1996 and 2004, foreign direct investment in Spain increased from €4 billion to €15 billion. A public deficit of almost 5 per cent of GDP was eliminated.[235] The number of people employed increased from 12.6 million to 17.6 million, of which the number of women employed increased from 4.3 million to 6.8 million. Unemployment came down, from 3.7 million to 2.3 million and long-term unemployment decreased from 2.1 million to 0.8 million. This successful economic development allowed health spending to rise from €530 per person to €950. Tourism increased from 35 million to 52 million foreign visitors a year. These improvements can also be seen in a doubling of the number of people who go to the theatre and strong increases in the number of books published and library visits. The environment improved in several ways, with forest areas increasing and the area dedicated to nature reserves doubling.[236]

So what did they do and how did they do it? There were a number of reforms to create stable macroeconomic conditions and also a series

---

[232] *The Economist* (2004b)

[233] *The Economist*

[234] *The Economist* (2004b)

[235] Eurostat (1996)

[236] Fundaciòn FAES (2006).

of structural reforms. State-owned gas, electricity, telecom and oil companies were privatised. The state's share of stock market capitalisation decreased from 11 per cent to 0.5 per cent. The marginal income tax rate was reduced from 56 per cent to 45 per cent and several taxes on smaller businesses were abolished. Many product markets were deregulated and financial markets made more transparent and efficient. Government was also decentralised, with more powers given to the regions.

Spain also used deregulation of the labour market, which had been extremely rigid under the Franco era, to introduce more flexibility. One main reform was the introduction in 1984 of part-time contracts that were not subject to the rigidities of the existing labour market. That led to a substantial increase in the number of people in temporary employment. In 1997, the government attempted to achieve an increase in permanent contracts by reducing payroll taxes and dismissal costs for permanent contracts. An increase in employment among the young was the main consequence.[237]

Spain has also been a receiver of EU Structural Funds and the effect of this inflow of income may be difficult to measure. One study suggests that between 1989 and 2006 it accounted for 0.56 percentage points of the annual growth in the recipient regions—a period when the national annual average growth rate was more than 3 per cent. It also suggests that the funds might explain 0.74 per cent of the fall in unemployment, a period when unemployment decreased from 22 per cent to 8.5 per cent.[238] Thus, the effect was positive but marginal, which should prompt questions about the funds considering the scope of funds received by Spain.

---

[237] Kugler, Jimeno-Serrano & Hernanz (2003).

[238] Sosvilla-Rivero (2005).

During the past decade, Spain has also become a country of immigration. In 1996, a mere 1.4 per cent of the population had a foreign nationality. In 2005, the figure was 8.4 per cent.[239] The number of non-EU foreign residents increased from 205,000 to 1,075,000 between 1996 and 2004.[240] These people have come largely from Africa and Latin America. During this immigration phase, unemployment was almost halved. How well integrated are these immigrants in the labour market? Research has showed that the immigrants initially showed higher participation rates, higher unemployment, higher incidence of over-qualification and higher incidence of temporary contracts. However, five years after their arrival, unemployment levels had come down to those of native Spaniards, though they more often work on temporary contracts.[241] Fully integrating such a large number of immigrants in the labour market is a remarkable achievement and since it has increased the number of working people, it has contributed substantially to Spain's national success.

Some lessons from Spain are that it is possible to succeed not only with economic reforms in general but also with substantial immigration. Furthermore, Spain confirms that a fairly large country can be reformed and that a shift of government does not lead to reforms being rolled back. The governments of José Maria Aznar had a main role in the reforms, which were mainly launched during his first term, in 1996–2000. Before him, however, the democratisation and normalisation of Spain was essential. Aznar has since summarised some of his conclusions:

"I have always held that the only policy worthy of the name is one based on ideas, convictions and principles. At the same time, I think that ideas

---

[239] Fernández & Ortega (2006).

[240] Fundaciòn FAES (2006).

[241] Fernández & Ortega (2006)

are not without their consequences: good ideas generate positive conse-
quences in terms of progress, whilst mistaken ideas provoke uncertainty,
problems, and finally lead to a deteriorating in living standards for indi-
viduals. So government is not only a question of administration, but also
of advocating and implementing ideals… And the future is in the ideas:
the ideas of a reformist centre."[242]

The current prime minister, José Luis Rodríguez Zapatero, has of course inherited a smoothly functioning economy, but there are future challenges. His government has taken a bold move to continue on the path of immigration and integration by deciding to granting an amnesty to illegal immigrants. Anyone who could prove they had worked in the country for more than six months was entitled to a permit to remain legally in the country. This has proven the largest amnesty reform ever undertaken in Europe: some 700,000 people applied for work permits in three months during 2005.[243] This move brought many people from the informal sector to the regular labour market.

Spain still needs more reform. There are immediate issues, like high house prices, but also long-term and structural issues to be faced. Unemployment is still fairly high, labour productivity rather low, the tax system is complex and tax evasion extensive, and the pension system is in great need of reform. In fact, pensions already consume some 50 per cent of state social expenditure and will in 2030 (if nothing is done) account for 80 per cent, which would leave rather little to other public services.[244] The OECD recommends reforms in unemployment protection for regular workers and more competition in

---

[242] Fundaciòn FAES (2006)

[243] Crawford (2005)

[244] Boeri (2004).

the retail sector.[245] The Zapatero government has committed itself to further reform.

The Empire Struck Back

No selection of countries that have successfully launched reforms in a difficult political climate can ignore the UK. In the late 1970s, the country was regarded as the sick man of Europe, with one of its lowest levels of GDP per capita. Economic data made for depressing reading, with double-digit inflation, low productivity and serious unemployment. Of course, this miserable state was mirrored in everyday life, with perhaps the most visible signs being persistent strikes, garbage in the streets, very low housing standards and poorly managed state-owned companies. Occasional outbreaks of rioting were seen on the streets of London. Total public spending exceeded 50 per cent of GDP and markets were highly regulated. At that time, nobody could have described Britain as a country with an "Anglo-Saxon hyper liberal" economic model. On the contrary, the country lagged behind West Germany on most counts. This underperformance excacerbated an identity crisis in the wake of the fall of the British Empire.

The current UK population stands at 61 million. GDP per capita is the seventh highest in the EU—which today has 27 member states—and the rate of unemployment is in the lower tier of EU states.[246] The UK is today the second largest recipient of foreign direct investment

---

[245] OECD (2007a).

[246] Eurostat, http://epp.eurostat.ec.europa.eu/pls/portal/docs/PAGE/PGP_PRD_CAT_PREREL/PGE_CAT_PREREL_YEAR_2007/PGE_CAT_PREREL_YEAR_2007_MONTH_08/3-31082007-EN-BP.PDF

[247] OECD (2007b).

in the entire OECD, surpassed only by the United States.[247] The City of London has overtaken New York as the world's leading financial centre in the world, generating one fifth of UK corporate tax revenue with a mere 350,000 employees. London today exerts a strong attraction. Some 600,000 citizens of the new EU member states since 2004 have come to work there which, by the way, has been estimated to have lifted UK GDP by an additional percentage point since then.

Nowhere in Europe do house prices come anywhere near the levels of central London. Many of the previously state-owned companies that persistently showed huge deficits—covered by taxpayers every year—became efficient global corporations, like British Airways.[248] Income inequality in the UK is among the highest in the OECD and EU, but the share of households with low income is low and has decreased substantially—from 40 per cent in 1990 to 18 per cent in 2004. All income levels have increased—the top ones more than the bottom ones, but all have increased.[249]

Not all politicians get an -ism of their own. Margaret Thatcher did with Thatcherism, which goes to show how groundbreaking her policies were at the time. The reforms that brought the UK back from the doldrums were launched during her period as prime minister from 1979 to 1990. Currency regulations were scrapped and the UK became the first country with free movement of capital. Inflation was brought under control, though it took some time, with a monetary policy set on that aim. A number of taxes were cut, with the top rate of income tax being reduced from 83 per cent to 40 per cent. Total public expenditure fell from 44 percent to 40.5 per cent of GDP. State-owned companies in the electricity, gas, steel, car manufacturing,

---

[247] OECD (2007b).

[248] *The Economist* (2007a)

[249] Euromonitor International (2006).

telecom and other sectors were sold to private investors. During the Thatcher years, the size of the nationalised industry sector was reduced by 60 per cent.

Labour market deregulation featured a number of measures, several of which were aimed at curbing trade union power. A new law forced municipalities to purchase all services that were not genuinely public goods in the private market. Competition was introduced in welfare provision and 95 per cent of all hospitals were transformed from public monopolies to private trusts. Financial markets were deregulated and a rather sleepy London Stock Exchange opened up to the world markets. Legislation made it possible for people in municipal housing to buy their homes and in ten years, municipal housing decreased from 32 per cent to 20 per cent of total housing. During the 1980s, the UK economy grew faster than that of any European country except Spain, foreign direct investment increased by more than in any OECD country except Japan, and between 1983 and 1990 more than 3 million new jobs were created.[250]

The UK has enjoyed continued economic success. After the international recession of the early 1990s, it has now had 14 consecutive years of substantial economic growth. The governments after Thatcher have accepted all the major changes implemented during those turbulent years. Though successive governments have again increased public spending as a percentage of GDP, they have also launched some new reforms. Under Tony Blair and Gordon Brown, the Bank of England was made independent. Some public service reforms have also been put in place, such as increased private funding for universities and use of public private partnerships in the provision and funding of public services.

---

[250] Thatcher (1993), *The Economist* (2007a), Norrmann & Stein (2006).

The main explanation for Britain's success over the past decade is arguably its openness and integration in the world economy—and previous reforms. Levels of trade in goods, foreign investments, financial trade and immigration are all very high. The UK is a central part of the booming global economy and has embraced rapid change with a flexible economy. It made no headlines at all that a car plant with thousands of employees closed down just before the last general election. Such events are normal, with the attitude being that new jobs will be created instead.

Contrary to most countries, including the United States, there is almost no debate about investors from Dubai, India, Germany and the Netherlands purchasing old British companies in steel, car and aircraft manufacturing. The Economist concluded: "Just as Britain led the world into industrialisation, so now Britain is leading it out. Today, you can still find a few British engineers and scientists making jet engines and pharmaceuticals and doing rather well at it. But many more are cooking up algorithms for hedge funds and investment banks—where in many cases they add more value... If foreigners think they can manage British factories or finances better than the natives can, they are welcome."[251]

In the 1960s and 1970s, most Western countries had been developing in the direction of a more "mixed economy", as it was called. State economic intervention was increasing in terms of taxes, regulation, spending and ownership. Communism in the East and socialism in the West were still alive and well enough to dominate politics. The UK was the first country to break with that development and reverse it. Countries may consider it hard to reform today. But whereas now many countries have successfully walked that path, back then no other

---

[251] *The Economist* (2007f).

country had. The Thatcher governments faced strong, persistent and sometimes violent opposition at home. And though politics is never as straightforward as it may be described afterwards, they held the course.

Reforms were defended and new reforms were launched. There was fierce resistance by special interests but the strength of public support surprised many commentators. The robustness of the reforms became an asset in elections.[252] This did not only change the UK but also many other Western countries which, sooner or later, became inspired by the reforms and their success. In fact, many of the reforms that back then were described as so revolutionary look quite mainstream nowadays, with the exception of labour market deregulation, which went further than in most other Western countries. The reform agenda, its influence and success also contributed to a transformation of the political landscape, making Social Democratic parties accept market economy.

The UK however faces challenges too and there are still many areas that have not yet been reformed. Public services fail to deliver at the level of quality demanded and health care waiting lists persist, despite more state funding. In recent years, taxes and public expenditure have been increasing, while the opposite has taken place in most other countries—a trend that will be harmful if allowed to continue.[253] The OECD recommends cutting taxes for low-income earners and reforms of infrastructure. The UK furthermore should implement measures to increase labour productivity to enable a further ascent up the production value chain.[254]

---

[252] Pirie (1988).

[252] *The Economist* (2007b).

[252] OECD (2007a), *The Economist* (2007f).

The UK offers many lessons. First, that it is possible to reform and transform relatively large OECD countries, not just small ones. Second, that reformers are often re-elected—Thatcher was re-elected three times and was followed by John Major, who achieved a fourth consecutive victory for the Conservative party. Third, the importance of ideas. During Thatcher's first years of opposition in 1974–1979, much energy was dedicated to developing well-founded, solid, detailed reform proposals that had a clear direction. The leading politicians co-operated with think-tanks like the Institute of Economic Affairs and Centre for Policy Studies and leading academics like Friedrich Hayek. This solid political content was essential to maintain direction and change society. Fourth, the British experience shows the need for strong political leadership, especially when faced with opposition. There may be strong special interests to be faced, but if done successfully the entire country will gain. Fifth, the UK example confirms that reforms are not rolled back even when there is a shift of government.

From Basket Case To Case Study

In geography class at school in Sweden, I was taught that New Zealand is exactly on the other side of the planet. Of course that means that it is very, very far away. Indeed, New Zealand can only count on Australia as a close neighbor. Now that Asia is booming and becoming a centre for global trade, New Zealand's relative isolation looks somewhat different compared to my first school days in the early 1980s. Back then, New Zealand had for a long time gone to great efforts to isolate itself from the rest of the world, with great problems as the consequence. With roots in the international economic crisis of the early 1930s, New Zealand had pursued protectionist policies to insulate itself from international economic fluctuations.

Thus, it was not only far away geographically but actually tried to distance itself economically from everyone else.

The decade before 1984 saw protectionism and state economic intervention reaching new heights. During that decade, public expenditure increased from 28 per cent of GDP to 39 per cent, economic growth was half the OECD average, unemployment increased twentyfold (albeit from low levels) and public debt soared. For the past 25 years, New Zealand's productivity growth had been the lowest in the OECD, which saw the country drop from third wealthiest in the world to number 23. The Australian prime minister at the time described New Zealand as a security risk to Australia. The state controlled prices, wages, rents and interest rates. It subsidised exports and had very high tariffs on imports, while product and financial markets were strictly regulated. From 1984, however, an economy that has been referred to as "the most interventionist outside the Third World and the Iron Curtain countries" went through what former OECD chief economist David Henderson described as "one of the most notable episodes of liberalisation that history has to offer".[255]

Contrary to the protectionist response to the economic crisis in the 1930s, New Zealand went far and fast in the opposite direction. From 1984 onwards, a raft of reforms were launched: a floating exchange rate was introduced, financial markets were deregulated, industry subsidies removed, tax rates cut and the tax base widened, the public deficit was cut, price controls were abolished, tariffs were cut, state-owned companies were privatised, training programmes for unemployed were introduced, welfare support was targeted to those in real need and monetary policy directed towards low inflation.

---

[255] More information can be found in Trotter (1996); Douglas (1998).

The number of public-sector employees dropped from 88,000 in 1984 to 34,000 in 1994.

A number of positive effects were seen from these reforms, which were carried out in two waves, in the mid-1980s and early 1990s. Having peaked at 44 per cent in 1991, public spending was down to 33 per cent by 1998. Productivity picked up and average annual economic growth since 1993 has been 3.7 per cent. Deficits became surpluses.[256]

The 1980s reforms were launched by the Labour party in government, re-elected once. It did not manage to make more than minor changes in the labour market, though. In the 1990 elections, the National party gained power and introduced comprehensive labour market reform. The Employment Contracts Act of 1991 (ECA) replaced compulsory unionism with freedom of association. The new contract did not mention trade unions, which had no privileges, and there was no bias for or against collective bargaining. Choice of contract was free and strikes or lockouts were only permitted if they related to negotiation of a new or expired contract for the employees concerned. Professor Charles Baird considered the reform "a bold, giant step towards the worthy goal of restoring freedom of contract to New Zealand labour markets".

Some aspects of the ECA went in the opposite direction, such as increased regulation of redundancies. But the overall effects were highly positive. Working days lost due to strikes fell from 266,000 a year in the five years before 1991 to 11,000 in 1998. Unemployment fell from 11 per cent in 1991 to 6 per cent in 1996 and to 3.6 per cent in 2004. The labour force participation rate is now 76 per cent, well

---

[256] Kerr (2005); Douglas (1998).

above the OECD average. And contrary to fears and criticism, average real wages did not fall due to the new, flexible, contracts.[257] In 2000 and 2004, some alterations were made by a new Labour government, though it is still too early to draw conclusions about their effects.

Some small steps had been initiated already before the new government took office in 1984, but that year was the breakthrough for reform. New Zealand was not the first country to reform but was one of those that enacted the most comprehensive and substantial reforms. Roger Douglas, who became finance minister in 1984 and has been praised as a main architect of the reform programme, has pointed out that one should never regard reforms in isolation. The improvements in the labour market, for example, cannot be attributed solely to the ECA but were also due to changes such as the introduction of a flatter tax, the reduction of top-rate income tax from 66 per cent to 33 per cent, the increased incentives to work, reductions in welfare benefits and changes in monetary policy that affected wage bargaining. He concludes that reforms should aim at increasing efficiency, improve the incentive structure and be practical and dynamic. Furthermore, Douglas stresses that a government should not compromise on reform in order to reach consensus but should implement comprehensive reform at high speed. Vested interests, he says, will always resist reform initially and accept it afterwards—and governments should seek credibility by clear consistency between policy and communication.[258]

New Zealand needs further reform. Considerable time has elapsed since the two successful reform waves and the positive effects are waning. GDP per capita is still below the OECD average, almost

---

[257] Kerr (2005)

[258] Douglas (1998).

entirely due to low productivity per hour. Further labour market liberalisation should be a priority. The OECD also recommends incentives to improve efficiency in the public sector, electricity market deregulation and improved education.[259] In a longer perspective, New Zealand of course faces the same challenges as other wealthy countries. These are best met with more flexibility, lower taxes and reform of welfare services and social security systems.

From Welfare to Work

The United States of America is a large and highly diverse country which, in many ways, is easier to compare with the whole of Europe rather than with single European countries. It covers an area similar to that of Europe and has 301 million inhabitants. This is not to say that there are not geographical, ethnic, economic or social differences within Spain or Denmark, but they are of an altogether different magnitude in the US. The US arouses feelings like few other countries and opinion polls in recent years have shown that people in large parts of the world have become more negative towards it.[260] There are reasons for this, though it is probably also true, as someone joked, that many anti-US demonstrators over the world would gladly accept a Green Card if they were offered one. An intense debate is ongoing about American failures and successes—in research as well as in the public debate. For every point made about success, someone will point to at least one failure, and vice versa. However, many people agree that economic growth, productivity and employment have all performed very well in the US. There is, though, one other issue that is worth studying in a reform context: welfare reform.

---

[259] OECD (2007a).
[260] The Pew Research Center (2007b).

Like any reform of complex systems, the Personal Responsibility and Work Opportunity Reconciliation Act signed by President Bill Clinton on 22 August 1996 had many different parts. The general background was that the incentives to leave public welfare benefits for work were not particularly strong for many poor people, leaving millions of people dependent on state benefits. There were also other—similar— disadvantages in previous tax and welfare systems: "One million people were on the welfare rolls because it was the only way they could get health care for their children," Clinton said.[261] The previous system had its main roots in President Lyndon Johnson's famous "War on Poverty" and the Aid to Families with Dependent Children (AFDC) programme. But instead of actually relieving poverty, it cemented it by creating dependency on government and the number of people in the system rose steadily from 1965 to 1994, peaking at 5 million.

The main elements of the welfare reforms were: ending the legal entitlement for welfare benefits; establishing time limits and work requirements to participate in the programme; and increasing the possibilities of states to decide other requirements. The AFDC was replaced by Temporary Assistance to Needy Families (TANF). The aim was described as making welfare "a second chance, not a way of life". The economic benefit from going to work for a woman with one child increased by 20 per cent and for a woman with two or more children it increased by 34 per cent. By making people go from welfare to work the reform also aimed to reduce child poverty. Access to public health care was linked to low income rather than living off public welfare. The separate decision in 1993 to undertake a major expansion of the earned income tax credit (that is, lower taxes for low-income earners) was also an important step that further

---

[261] Clinton (2004).

increased incentives to work. In the early 1990s, individual states launched similar welfare reforms. Following the federal reform, many states chose to cut benefits, introduce welfare-to-work programmes and part-subsidise some jobs. The 1996 reform required able people to go to work after two years on welfare and there were provisions to make sure that people did not become worse off from working.[262]

The changes were quite fundamental and the reform controversial. In fact, Clinton had vetoed two previous versions of the 1996 welfare reform bill, launched by the Republicans in Congress. Opponents in the public debate painted a dark picture of the future after welfare reform. One critic argued that "wages will go down, families will fracture, millions of children will be made more miserable than ever". A senator claimed that "hungry and homeless children" would be "begging for money, begging for food". The Nation magazine argued that "people will die, businesses will close, infant mortality will soar".[263]

The effects proved to be quite the opposite. Since 1996, the number of people on public welfare has fallen by 56 per cent. According to Department of Health and Human Services statistics, the number of children in poverty decreased by 1.6 million between 1995 and 2004. In the 1990s, employment among single mothers increased by nearly 50 per cent and among young single mothers (18–24) by nearly 100 per cent. Poverty among black children has fallen faster than any time before records began and reached the lowest levels ever. Many people who left welfare benefits for work did at first get a fairly low entry-level wage, but studies conclude that they have gained experi-

---

[262] Blank (2004); Clinton (2004).

[263] Tanner (2006).

ence and increased their wages. Manpower Demonstration Research Corporation has shown that people who move from welfare to work are optimistic, believing that their lives will be better in one to five years.[264]

As with all reforms, it is difficult to know for sure what actually caused the outcome. Can the quite massive improvements really be attributed to welfare reform or did the generally positive economic development cause them? Of course, a growing economy helps. But during economic expansions in the 1960s and 1970s, the number of people on welfare benefits actually increased. And despite the economic slowdown in the US in the early 2000s, the number of people on welfare benefits has remained low. One study attributed three quarters of the reduction in welfare benefits and increase in employment to the reform and one quarter to the general economic development.[265] Another study has found evidence of a strong positive correlation between state welfare reforms with strong work incentives and the rise in income for poor families and for single parents.[266]

The US welfare reforms offer a number of lessons. One is that incentives work. Cuts in taxes and welfare benefits will improve employment and incomes—and reduce poverty. Another lesson is that it is indeed possible to change a large public welfare program, in a large country too. A third lesson is that there might be loud opponents of a reform and widespread fears beforehand, but if the reform is implemented and the results are visible then opposition will fade and reformers will gain recognition. A politically strategic lesson might be that Clinton largely adopted a proposal from his political

---

[264] Figures and facts from Kim & Rector (2006); Blank (2004); Tanner (2006).

[265] June E. O'Neill and M. Anne Hill, Gaining Ground? Measuring the Impact of Welfare Reform on Welfare and Work, Manhattan Institute Civic Report No. 17, July 2001

[266] Blank & Schoeni (2003).

opponents, placing him in the political centre and depriving his opponents of substantial parts of their content and thereby their arguments for gaining power.

The Big Three

With a combined population of 204 million, Germany (82.5 million), France (63.5 million) and Italy (58 million) are undoubtedly the heavyweights of Continental Europe. They have half the population of the euro-zone. They are also the main founding countries behind the European Union, with a particularly strong, decades-long axis between Germany and France. Though Germany and Italy did not unite as nation states until the 19th century, they all have had leading roles throughout European history and have a massive historic, cultural and political heritage. For several decades after World War II, they all had impressive economic performance, quickly approaching the GDP per capita level of the US. For the past 10–20 years, however, they have lagged behind and experienced increasing economic problems. Despite the need for reforms, quite little has happened in these big three European countries. They are commonly cited as the essence of European economic problems, the "eurosclerosis", and the inability of wealthy countries to reform despite problems and rising future challenges.

Why mention Germany, France and Italy among countries that have come far? Surely they belong in the opposite group? True. Several smaller countries have done more than these three but are not mentioned. However, it is important to show that even the countries that have seemed unable to reform have actually done things. They should just do a lot more of the same. In that task, they can build on historic success. After all, the German "Wirtschaftswunder" was largely a consequence of a relatively free economy. These three countries are in fact in better positions to launch substantial reforms than several other nations before, which managed to turn things around. The UK in the late 1970s was in a much worse state—and there were no other reformist countries to learn from, which is the case today.

The German economy used to be the engine of Europe. But an increasing burden of taxes, social benefits and regulation gradually stalled it. Other explanations include inflexible corporatism, lack of competition and poor schools. The policies following the reunification of Germany in 1990 also put a heavy burden on the Bundesländer in the west (so far, they have sent €1.3 trillion to the east). In fact, the five eastern Bundesländer are a perfect example of what happens if a country leaves a centrally planned economy without introducing substantial free-market reforms and instead becomes dependent on foreign aid. Both payers and receivers suffer.

In the 1990s, the German engine had almost stopped, with unemployment reaching unprecedented levels and growth approaching zero. Chancellor Helmut Kohl had tried to pursue reforms but faced resistance from the opposition SPD, which then controlled the second chamber of parliament. Once in government, his successor Gerhard Schröder launched the Agenda 2010 reform package, containing some tax cuts, increased labour market flexibility and lower unemployment benefits. The reforms were modest, introduced piecemeal and partly watered down—but some things were achieved.[267] Schröder's ultimate failure was not the content of the reform but the political strategy, which was lacking in communication, packaging and timing.[268]

---

[267] *The Economist* (2006a).
[268] Posen (2005b).

In the last few years the German economy has picked up and exports in particular have increased. Germany's exports have risen by 40 per cent more than France's for the past ten years and the country is now the world's largest exporter. The absolute increase is partly cyclical and due to the international economic boom, but the relative increase is probably partly due to reform. One main reason is surely the substantial cost-cutting that has taken place in German business, without political involvement. Trade unions agreed with employers to longer working hours and thus lower wages per hour. In fact, German relative unit costs in 2006 were 90 per cent of their level in 2000. The equivalent figures for France and Italy are 97.5 per cent and 121 per cent respectively.[269] Corporate tax rates have also been cut, from 43 to 34 per cent, further reducing costs.[270] The decreased cost base for German industry in turn boosted the country's global competitiveness. This naturally does not eradicate the need for further long-term reform in Germany, but high costs were a particular and persistent problem.[271] The labour market agreement to cut costs is quite remarkable. Trade unions clearly felt a sense of responsibility, realising that without a competitive industry the prospects for jobs and living standards for ordinary people looked bleak.

Since France has more tourists than any country in the world, most people know that it is a beautiful country with a proud tradition. But occasional visitors to the banlieues of Paris will see the need for change. France has come to be seen as the European country that is the most resistant to reform. The political defence of the traditional social model against everything from globalisation to Polish plumbers has been quite fierce. The rhetoric of former president Jacques Chirac and his last prime minister, Dominique de Villepin, was protectionist

---

[269] OECD (2007c).
[270] Riches-Flores (2007).
[271] Posen (2005a).

and hostile to change in general. This style of communication might partly be explained by French political tradition, but there was also an amount of real protectionist policy content.

The traditional model was defended despite quite serious problems that have repeatedly led to riots—something that would normally be interpreted as a need for change rather than the opposite. French governments even introduced harmful new labour market regulations like the 35-hour week, in stark contrast to Germany's cost-cutting labour market agreements, and intervened to block corporate mergers. The election of Nicolas Sarkozy as president and the mandate confirmed by his party gaining a clear majority in parliament may signify a different form of leadership. Sarkozy promised "protection" but also quick and bold reform. Perhaps, in a decade, the least reformist European country will be in a rather different position.[272]

France displays both counter-reforms and failed reform attempts. Jacques Chirac himself failed in his reform attempts in the late 1980s and so did his government led by Alain Juppé in 1995. But some reforms did take place in the mid-1980s. For example, subsidies to the shipbuilding industry were cut and thousands of people had to be laid off. Alain Madelin, then industry minister, handled the difficult transformation. To defuse criticism, he directed some of the subsidies as compensation to the people laid off, who were helped to start new businesses, and free enterprise zones with more favourable conditions for entrepreneurship were created.[273] In 2005, France also introduced a new law for companies with fewer than 20 employees, where the trial employment period was prolonged to two years during which the employer can lay off an employee for any reason (at all).

---

[272] *The Economist* (2006b).

[273] Madelin (2007).

But as a similar proposal for the young was proposed, millions of people arranged demonstrations with signs demanding "Regulation!", despite a youth unemployment at 22 per cent—and eventually the government withdrew it.[274] Clearly, it is not sufficient to have substantial problems for reforms to be effectively launched. But the first law, for smaller businesses, with the new contract called CNE, was a notable deregulation, though, of course, it had a distortive effect since it was partial. France serves as an example that governments cannot reform by stealth, that politicians cannot communicate protection and implement partial deregulation and that once you give in to demonstrators, you have lost. But the shipbuilding lesson also offers strategic lessons about how to handle opposition successfully.

Italy is a great place to visit, with its historical monuments, lively atmosphere, hospitable climate and excellent food. But it has become the new "sick man of Europe", with a number of economic problems and serious future challenges. Economic growth has been the lowest in Europe for years and the effects are becoming visible amid creaking infrastructure and stagnating incomes. Public debt is 120 per cent of GDP and employment rates are the lowest in Western Europe.[275] Italy's birthrate is the lowest in Europe at 1.3 children per woman on average. If there are no pension and other reforms, the labour force will drop from 39 million in 2000 to a mere 22 million in 2050.[276] The economy performed well for decades after World War II, which meant that the country suffered little economically from the fact that governments usually could not stay in office for a full term. But for 15 years at least, long-term reformist political leadership has been needed. This need has proven difficult to meet. One oft-cited reason

---

[274] Norrmann & Stein (2006).

[275] *The Economist* (2005c).

[276] Stein & Reading (2003).

for this is a lack of trust in the state and in government among ordinary Italians.

However, during the governments of Silvio Berlusconi Italy did carry out important pension reforms, raising the retirement age, encouraging private pension funds and cutting the value of state pensions. Given its level of public debt and demographics, Italy still has to do more in the same direction. But the Berlusconi initiatives serve as a start which hopefully later governments will not reverse.

The most substantial reforms to date have been seen in the labour market. The very low levels of employment, particularly among the young, and the extensive hidden economy, were the main reasons for launching the Biagi reform[277] to allow more flexible part-time jobs exempted from ordinary labour market regulations. The Biagi reform also opened up for private job agencies, made apprenticeship contracts more flexible, created new job contracts and introduced more flexibility for outsourcing.

The reform was launched in 2001 and implemented from 2003, with regional differences.[278] Former labour minister Maurizio Sacconi has claimed that Italy created a net 1.2 million new jobs during 2000–2005.[279] Indeed, Italian unemployment has decreased from well above the EU average of 8.4 per cent as late as 2001 to 6.8 per cent in 2006 (compared to the EU average in 2006 of 7.9 per cent).[280] The Biagi reform was very controversial in Italy. Its main advisor, Mr Biagi, was assassinated and anti-reform demonstrations drew more than

---

[277] The reform is described in some detail in Tiraboschi (2006a).

[278] Tiraboschi (2006b).

[279] *The Economist* (2005c).

[280] Eurostat (1996).

1 million people onto the streets of Rome. Nevertheless, the government stayed the course.

These are interesting reforms, yet much more needs to be done. It might also be necessary to point out that reform is not about Germany, France and Italy adopting some foreign—"Anglo-Saxon" or other—concept of society. The origins and ideas of wealth creation can be found all over Europe: in the first free-trading Italian city-states, in the forceful arguments by Frenchman Frédéric Bastiat, in the works by Scottish philosopher Adam Smith, Germany's Ludwig Erhard, and the Austrians like Ludwig von Mises and Friedrich Hayek. Indeed, it all started in Europe and for Germany, France and Italy, it is more about re-discovering the European origins once partially abandoned. Why should people in other parts of the world necessarily be better at adopting the ideas and practice of that European legacy today?

Two Tales of Health Care

While many countries have implemented far-reaching reforms of monetary and trade policy and product markets and tax systems, few have managed to change health care. In most OECD countries, it is still largely tax-funded and usually also provided by the state—or its local levels. There are problems and many studies have shown what reforms could and should do. And in an increasingly service-oriented society, with rising demand for health services, there is no need for health care not to be a modern, growing industry that attracts talents and delivers high-quality services on time. Several countries have undertaken more limited reforms, such as introducing more competition among providers. But two—Switzerland and the Netherlands—have pursued a different model. Both have large privately funded health care sectors and have introduced competition on a major scale. They also offer other reform lessons.

Switzerland is one of the world's richest nations, and has been so for most of the 20th century. It is known for its romantic villages, high-quality watches and successful banks. With 7.5 million inhabitants, it has four official languages. It is not a member of the European Union and was not even a member of the United Nations until a few years ago. In many ways, it is an exceptional country—very open to the world and a very decentralised federation that has to hold a referendum every time the federal government wants to take new initiatives. Public expenditure is only 30 per cent of GDP, though it has been rising rapidly, and growth rates have been modest for a number of years.[281] Still, Switzerland's system of internal tax competition between the 26 cantons keeps taxes low and competitive.[282] The Swiss are also among those who are the most content with their health care system.

At 11.5 per cent of GDP, Switzerland devotes more money to health care than any other OECD country except Luxembourg and the United States. It has the third highest life expectancy in the world after Japan and San Marino.[283] Only about 55 per cent of health care is publicly funded, reflecting the existence of a law making it mandatory for people to have private health care insurance. Such insurance is purchased from one of roughly 100 insurance companies that such coverage (usually those that operate in the policyholder's home canton). A number of voluntary private health care insurance policies are also available to complement basic insurance. On top of the insurance premiums, there are fees to be paid. Swiss health care is of

---

[281] *The Economist* (2004a).

[282] An accessible account of this can be found in Bessard (2007).

[283] The World Health Organisation (b).

very high quality but nevertheless has significantly lower costs than in the United States.[284] There is a high degree of consumer choice, which leads to competition. In recent years, costs have been rising, however, and there is criticism of an absence of incentives for cost control. Some analysts have perceived a problem in respect of adverse selection, and changes have been proposed to correct that.[285] The system is not perfect (no system ever can be) but its foundation on private insurance and private health-care provision solves some of the problems experienced by countries in relation to a lack of choice, competition and funding.

With its strong trade and commercial traditions, the Netherlands was one of Europe's wealthiest countries for a long time too. But in the 1970s it experienced serious economic trouble following a vast expansion of taxes and welfare benefits. This was the so-called Dutch disease, meaning welfare without work. In 1982, the trend was broken following a deal between business and trade unions in Wassenaar, a suburb of The Hague, that has been seen as the Dutch corporatist "polder model" at work. Wage bargaining became more decentralised, a stronger emphasis was placed on jobs and trade unions agreed to wage restraint.

The government embarked on a course of sorting out the macroeco- nomic imbalances and cutting taxes. The top rate of income tax was cut from 72 to 52 per cent. Wim Kok, a trade union leader in 1982, later became a reformist prime minister. Governments during the 1990s also pursued reforms, such as trimming welfare benefits, under then-prime minister Ruud Lubbers. In the 1980s and 1990s, public debt dropped and growth increased to 3 per cent on average

---

[284] OECD, Reviews of Health Systems, 2006.

[285] Civitas (2002).

annually for two decades. Employment has increased from 52 per cent to 74 per cent since 1982.[286] In recent years, the pace of the advances seems to have slowed down and new reforms are now called for. But the Netherlands did achieve a considerable amount during the timeframe in question.

One of the most recently enacted reforms is a completely new system of health care funding. From 2006, the 16.5 million Dutch have a new health care system under a law requiring citizens to buy health care insurance privately. The funding system has three main components: a private fee paid by the citizen; a state-funded fee of 6.5 per cent of the citizen's income (up to a maximum of €2,000 per year); and complementary funding from employers or fees for entrepreneurs. The average fee for an individual is about €1,000 euro a year and amounts to to 45 per cent of health care funding. If one does not use health care services for more than €225 a year, part of the fee is paid back as a rebate. People aged under 18 pay nothing. Complementary private insurance exists for special health care services like psychotherapy. Insurance companies provide health care from private clinics. The individual can change to another insurance company once a year and the number of people who have utilised this opportunity has exceeded expectations. Half of all citizens have group insurance, usually provided by their employer. Subsidies are made available to people on low incomes. The primary aims of the reform were to empower health care consumers and to increase choice and competition (and hence efficiency). The new system was introduced overnight for all citizens and evaluations so far have been very positive.[287]

---

[286] *The Economist* (2002).

[287] See, for example Bartholomée & Maarse (2006).

Contrary to common perceptions, it is possible to carry out substantial health care reforms and to introduce choice, competition and private funding. The oft-mentioned risks of adverse selection are manageable, as the Dutch example shows. It has been claimed that the difference between paying taxes to a public health care monopoly and purchasing mandatory private insurance is small. But there are two main differences: the latter offers choice, thereby stimulating competition and efficiency, and sets off a new dynamic in the system which might pave the way for further reform. From a political perspective, Jan-Peter Balkenende was re-elected as prime minister in 2006, though with a differently composed government coalition.

Conflicting Models

Last but not least, my home country Sweden, naturally the one I know the best. It is, in many ways, a fabulous country: modern, high-quality, technological and beautiful. All Swedes are proud of Ikea, Björn Borg and Ingmar Bergman. From time to time, the "Swedish model" is internationally discussed as something to emulate. The definition of that term is unclear and tends to vary over time. In the 1960s, it sometimes referred to the alleged "Swedish sin" and female liberation, and sometimes it referred to the rapid growth of the public sector. Lately, in the economic and political sense, it has aimed at telling a story of Swedish success and attempted to explain why it happens. Like all countries, Sweden has advantages and disadvantages, and it is of course essential for other countries to emulate the policies that lead to success rather than policies that hold back progress and create problems. Two Swedish reforms from which a number of conclusions can be drawn are particularly worth studying: school vouchers and pension reform.

A brief historic account shows that from 1890 to 1950 Sweden had one of the world's highest economic growth rates. Though levels remained high during the 1950s and 1960s, a number of other countries also experienced very strong growth, which meant that Sweden began to decline in relative terms.[288] During that long period of exceptional growth, Sweden went from being one of Europe's poorest nations to one of the wealthiest. This was largely a consequence of economic liberalisations in the 1860s and 1870s led by finance minister Johan August Gripenstedt. Total Swedish tax pressure increased from below 10 per cent of GDP in 1890 to only 20 per cent of GDP in 1950—lower than in the United States.[289] In the early 20th century, Sweden was a country of innovators and entrepreneurs, like Alfred Nobel and Lars Magnus Ericsson. The significance of that period is underlined by the fact that of the 50 largest Swedish companies today, only one has been founded after 1970 and most are about a century old. In the 1970s, Sweden experienced economic problems. These were triggered by the oil crisis but had deeper roots, and by the end of that decade total tax pressure as a share of GDP had reached almost 50 per cent of GDP. After 1968, there had been a wave of new state intervention in the economy, with more market regulation, payment of subsidies to old companies and nationalisation of others. Inflation and unemployment soared and growth plummeted. [290]

Then, from the late 1980s to mid-1990s there was a period of reform, first by the Social Democratic government led by Ingvar Carlsson and then, in particular, by the centre-right government of Carl Bildt. In the late 1980s, several product markets were deregulated, as were financial markets. A tax reform introduced broader tax bases and a top marginal tax rate of 50 per cent, down from 80 per cent. During

---

[288] Andersson-Skog & Krantz, eds (2002).

[288] Johansson (2004).

[288] Feldt (1991).

the Bildt government of 1991 to 1994, state-owned companies were sold, inflation kept low, school choice introduced, product markets further deregulated, subsidies to housing cut, tax rates decreased and Swedish EU membership negotiated. Some reforms, like the granting of independence to the central bank and pension reform, were initiated before 1994 but implemented later. Growth levels picked up and have for ten years now been above the EU average. Sweden became a centre for IT and telecoms following deregulation, foreign trade almost doubled as a share of GDP, inflation remained low and public debt dropped.

The reformist period coincided with an international recession combined with a domestic economic crisis following the problems that accumulated in the 1970s and 1980s. The public perception was that reform was connected to crisis, which is one reason why little has happened in the last decade. However, 2006 saw the election of a new four-party, centre-right coalition. This was remarkable since the parties were elected on the promise of change despite a growing economy. A key explanation for this is the fact that they managed to focus the debate and election on the main are where serious problems persist—the labour market.[291] Though the official Eurostat figure of unemployment in 2006, 7.1 per cent, did not seem too dramatic, many people who would have been unemployed were hidden in other parts of the vast Swedish welfare system, labelled as early retired, on sick leave, or similar. McKinsey Global Institute estimated Sweden's real total unemployment rate to be between 15 per cent and 17 per cent.[292] Thus, the current government is now pursuing labour market reforms with lower income taxes, lower payroll taxes and stricter unemployment benefits. In addition, it is selling off more

---

[291] Schenström (2007).

[292] McKinsey Global Institute (2006).

state-owned companies and introducing competition in health care. Some of the areas that were not reformed in the previous reform period are now in focus.

In 1993, Sweden introduced school choice by means of school vouchers. The school system is formally run by local municipalities, though all schools have to follow a national plan on educational content and formats. The voucher system essentially implied that a student received from his or her municipality 85 per cent of the sum that he or she would cost to educate in a state school. The student could then choose to attend any school, including private ones. Private schools that receive public funding via the voucher cannot demand private fees on top. The proportion of children attending private primary schools quadrupled in ten years and the same increase was seen among high school students. The levels are still low and differ widely between regions. In Stockholm, the proportion is about 15 per cent, whereas in some rural areas it is zero. Costs also differ widely between regions, being three times higher in some places than others. This is likely to be an issue of efficiency more than anything else. Several studies have shown positive effects on quality—in state schools as well—following the introduction of competition.[293] One survey found that an increase of 10 percentage points in the proportion of students attending private schools raises average pupil achievement by almost 1 percentile rank point. It also concluded that no group has lost from an increase in the proportion of students attending private schools. There is evidence of some segregation, but the over-represented pupils in private schools are not only those with well educated parents but also immigrants too.[294]

---

[293] Sandström & Bergström (2002).
[294] Böhlmark & Lindahl (2007).

School vouchers had been preceded by choice within the state system but the opportunity to choose a private school was controversial. Opponents thought it would cause segregation and that only the rich would choose the better schools. There was also resistance from municipal politicians from all parties. The then under-secretary of state for education, Odd Eiken, has pointed to a number of necessary strategic steps. First, agreeing to only provide 85 per cent of the cost, partly implying that private schools must be more efficient than public schools. Second, make the issue more pragmatic than ideological, also in order to defuse ideological differences within the government coalition. Third, allow the National School Board to monitor quality. Eiken also points to an existing pressure on the issue originating in the work of international think-tanks.[295] The Social Democratic government that came to power in 1994 did not dismantle the school voucher reform despite earlier fierce criticism, partly because of the resistance of the newly formed Swedish Association of Independent Schools.[296]

State pension systems are long-term contracts between generations that take a long time to change fundamentally. When Sweden introduced the first state pension system, in 1913, the retirement age was 57 and life expectancy was 55. In the late 20th century, retirement age had crept down to 59 and life expectancy had risen to 80.[297] Naturally, then, the system had become more expensive over the years. In 1959, Sweden introduced a pay-as-you-go pension system in a highly politicised battle where the Social Democrats won by one vote in parliament. The so-called ATP system became one of the most generous public pension systems in the world and a key symbol for the Social Democratic project of the time. The Swedish system, where generations of tomorrow were required to pay the pensions of today's

---

[295] Eiken (2007).

[296] The Swedish Association of Independent Schools, website.

[297] Westerberg (2000).

workers when they retire, proved economically unsustainable. The benefits far exceeded the payments. This was realised already in the 1970s, and in the 1980s committees worked on analyses to provide possible solutions. In 1991, the centre-right government invited the opposition Social Democrats to talks about a pension reform. A group of party representatives worked until 1994, when a principal agreement about a reform was reached. The Social Democrats needed no fewer than three party congresses—in 1992, 1994 and 1997—to get a mandate from its members to back the reform. After that, the reform was implemented.[298]

Though politically framed as a reform of the previous system, it is in effect a whole new system. Individual contributions are tied to the benefits. It is more of a funded system than pay-as-you-go. Retirement age is flexible and 2.5 percentage points of the 18.5 per cent paid from the individual's salary to the system is a so-called premium that he or she is allowed to invest in mutual funds. About 70 per cent of eligible Swedes exercised the right to actively invest those 2.5 per cent in the first year of the new system, choosing between 650 funds.[299] Public pension levels were cut by on average almost 40 per cent. Above that, there are private pensions based on deals between employers and employees, and above that, many people have private pension plans.

The reform has been called groundbreaking—how was it possible? It took place without a single protest and without a serious crisis. First of all, there was a genuine and well established knowledge among all experts that the old system was unsustainable. And the broad political majority working for a reform made it possible for both

[298] Kangas, Lundberg & Ploug (2006).

[298] Palme, Sundén & Söderlind (2005).

sides to look like they were fighting for their respective values. Special interests of all sorts were kept far away from the process. The Conservative representative in the parliamentary pension group, Margit Gennser, claims she was inspired by ideas from think-tanks like the Cato Institute.[300] Finally, the Social Democrats only secured the approval of party members after they had asked whether they were ready to break the preliminary agreement with the other parties, undoing all the work that had been done and making the party look unserious.[301]

Summary and Conclusions

A number of OECD countries have accomplished a great deal in the reform arena. The results have been very positive. The most far-reaching reforms have taken place in trade, product markets, macroeconomic frameworks and taxes. But contrary to some beliefs, several countries have also substantially reformed labour markets, pensions, schools, immigration laws and health care. Crises sometimes trigger reforms, but some countries can end up in crisis and still not reform—and some can reform without a crisis. European Union Structural Funds may have contributed positively in some countries, but they explain only a fraction of the success. In all countries, reforms have been stepwise and they have usually faced initial resistance—but all are accepted afterwards. The reformers have had a vision and direction—and they have been re-elected in almost all countries, at least once. Governments labelled left and right alike have both pushed for reforms. Efforts by independent institutes as well as public committees have been relevant for the creation of policy proposals.

---

[300] Gennser (2007).
[301] Kangas, Lundberg & Ploug (2006).

THE POLITICAL ARENA

"The ideas of economists and political philosophers, both when they are right and when they are wrong, are more powerful than is commonly understood. Indeed the world is ruled by little else. Practical men, who believe them selves to be quite exempt from any intellectual influence, are usually the slave of some defunct economist."

JOHN MAYNARD KEYNES[302]

"Society's course will be changed only by a change in ideas. First you must reach the intellectuals, the teachers and writers, with reasoned argument. It will be their influence on society that will prevail, and the politicians will follow."

FRIEDRICH HAYEK[303]

"Politics is the art of looking for trouble, finding it everywhere, diagnosing it incorrectly, and applying the wrong remedies."

GROUCHO MARX

A NUMBER OF COUNTRIES HAVE successfully launched substantial reforms. There is widespread knowledge of what could be done to improve growth, incomes, employment, welfare services, social security and general living standards. But why have the lessons from the reformist countries not spread like grass-fires among all the OECD countries? Why are countries not learning to a greater extent from

---

[302] Keynes (1936).
[303] Blundell (2005).

the success of others and initiating similar reforms? Of course no politician will know everything—there is always a lack of insight[304]—but the information is overwhelmingly there. Improvements in society are mainly created by people other than politicians—entrepreneurs, investors, workers—but politicians set many conditions for those that make the improvements happen. Therefore, in the end, substantial reform demands political action to tear down harmful barriers to change, progress and wealth creation. An understanding of what actually determines whether politicians will pursue reformist policies or not demands a look into the political system.

Much can be learned from the conditions that led to reforms in countries that accomplished a great deal and how governments actually went from knowledge to action. Every country needs reforms, some more than others. Considering the need for reform and the knowledge about what to do, very little is happening. Serious problems that have been solved in one country remain in many others—why? What in the political arena explains that? What are the conflicts, the problems, the stakeholders, the issues and the incentives? Only by understanding that can one see a pattern and cease to regard politics as irrational; it just follows its own rationality. That is also the only way, in the end, to know what the political rationality *for* reform might be.

A number of factors will affect whether reform takes place. Some lie within the political system and others can be found elsewhere in society. It has been said that "good policies are good politics".[305] But surprisingly often, good policies that would improve living standards for everyone do not become politics. Jean-Philippe Cotis, chief

---

[304] Berggren (2003).
[305] José Piñera, quoted in Rodrik (1996).

economist at the OECD, has asked: "At the end of the day, why does good practice not always spread to countries where policy changes are badly needed?"[306] The reform policies may be very controversial. A reform landscape surrounds the political arena and will affect whether ideas lead to change or not. These factors may be regarded as obstacles to reform or just features of society that a reformer must take into account. Any politician has to analyse the landscape and manoeuvre in it. The forces that operate in this landscape can be handled more or less successfully. But they exist and cannot be ignored.

A number of questions have to be addressed. What are the main features of the political arena? Where do policy ideas come from? How do ideas end up on the political agenda? How does the policy process work in reality? How is politics different from markets? What are the main features of the reform landscape?

Voters and Psychology

"While the history of market-based reforms has repeatedly shown that free markets, open trade and an economy fuelled by private ownership are enormously powerful in stimulating rapid economic growth, the general public rarely knows it or believes it at the start."[307]

These words of Jeffrey Sachs probably encapsulate the perceived puzzle quite well. One issue is of course how much people actually know about society, economics and politics. But there is also an issue of how we act, regardless of our degree of factual knowledge and insight. In economics, people are often assumed to be rational actors with fixed

---

[306] Cotis, Jean-Philippe, Editorial in OECD (2007a).

[307] Sachs Jeffrey, in Williamson, ed (1994).

preferences. In real life, this is often not the case. Research in the psychology of risk provides a few pieces of information that may clarify the situation and presents some strategic implications for politicians.

Consider facing two separate decisions. Decision one involves a choice between a sure gain of $240 and a 25 per cent chance of gaining $1,000. Decision two involves a choice between a sure loss of $750 and a 75 per cent risk of losing $1,000. Those choices were presented to a large group of respondents. How did people respond? In decision one, 84 per cent of respondents chose the sure gain of $240, not taking the chance. A computer would have chosen to take the chance, since 25 per cent of $1,000 is more than $240 anyway. In decision two, however, 87 per cent chose the risk of losing $1,000.[308] Thus, in the case of a sure but small gain, people chose it. But in the case of a sure loss, people chose to take the risk of losing even more— despite the fact that in both cases the likelihood of possible gain or possible risk is similar. This provides evidence that we do not take a risk if we want to gain something and we are anxious not to make a sure loss. We know what we have, and we do not want to lose it.

Another aspect has been refereed to as "mental accounting". Consider another choice, also presented to a large number of respondents. Imagine in case one that you have already paid $20 for a theatre ticket but you lose the ticket. The question is, would you buy a new ticket? In case two, you go to the theatre intending to purchase a ticket for $20 but discover on the way that you have lost a $20 note. Would you still pay $20 for a ticket? Clearly, in both cases, the economic outcome of a yes would be $40. Yet only 46 per cent of respondents said yes in case one, whereas 88 per cent said yes in case two.[309] The explanation

---

[308] Tversky (1990).
[309] Tversky (1990).

may be that we do a sort of mental accounting and that in the first case $20 had already been deducted from the mental "theatre account". But in case two, it was just a general economic loss and the "theatre account" was not credited. This indicates how we commonly structure our private economy. People may save for a holiday trip and borrow money for a new car—despite the interest rate on the borrowed money being higher than the trip savings, thus creating an economic loss. One might call this irrational, but it is the way we act.

It is not difficult to imagine policy consequences of priorities like trying to keep what we have and avoiding losses—or seemingly odd policy priorities due to mental accounting. There is a bias towards the current situation and against taking the risk of change, however certain the positive outcome may be. Of course, our behaviour in the capacity of voters may contain similar elements. Professor Bryan Caplan has provided some replies to the question of, in his terminology, "why democracies choose bad policies". It is sometimes assumed that a democratic system automatically leads to decisions that will improve the general good of society. His research shows that voters have a number of very strong beliefs with weak factual foundations and that are often incorrect, but that voters are still confident in embracing these misconceptions and pursuing them politically. He has divided these into three main misconceptions: that most voters do not understand the market economy and underestimate its effects; that most voters underestimate the benefits of interaction with foreigners; and that most voters wrongly equate prosperity with employment instead of with production. A combination of misconceptions and strong opinions—which will ultimately decide voting behaviour—might of course contribute to harmful policies in the end.[310]

---

[310] Caplan (2007).

When people act individually or in voluntary co-operation, they will largely bear the consequences of their actions themselves. But when people act in the capacity of voters, they influence the collective decision-making and what the state will be doing. Winston Churchill remarked that democracy "is the worst form of government, except all other forms that have been tried from time to time".[311] There will never be something such as a perfectly rational voter with full knowledge of everything. We have universal suffrage because it must be a fundamental right to have equal formal influence on the collective decisions by the state, since any political power is delegated from the citizens to the state. But voting may be irrational and based on misconceptions, and collective decisions in a democracy can be harmful to the public good. That is also one reason why all OECD countries have a representative democracy with limits on political power, balancing institutions and free media. A pluralistic society with a dynamic public debate improves the quality of policies and limits the scope of political power, thus limiting the possible adverse consequences of policies.

Which lessons does this provide for reformist politicians? Risk aversion means that broad popular support for change is generally unlikely, despite a need for change. Misconceptions mean that voters may not always know which reforms would be the best at the time, though they may agree with reforms afterwards. OECD chief economist Jean-Philippe Cotis has summarised the challenge, based on OECD research: "The costs of reform are fairly quick, but the results are more long-term. The costs are usually focused on specific, well-organised, groups of citizens. But the benefits are more general, they will improve all of society."[312] Thus, there will be loud voices defend-

---

[311] Eigen & Siegel (2003).

[312] Cotis, Jean-Philippe, Lecture, Confederation of Swedish Enterprise, 9 July, 2007.

ing the current order. Few, however, will argue for a change with future benefits that are not entirely measurable and certain. This presents obstacles to reform. Politicians who want to reform will always have to overcome initial resistance and misconceptions. Waiting for a general desire for change before acting will most likely turn out to be an eternal delay.

Political Incentives

When a person acts as a consumer or businessman in the market he or she will most likely pursue his or her self-interest. The voluntary transactions in the market, following free choice and competition, will usually benefit the common good. Sometimes this may not be the case, which is referred to as externalities or market failures. An example might be when a million people are contributing to pollution and the benefits for one person to cease polluting will hardly be noticed, so everyone continues. A voluntary deal between them all to quit is very unlikely to arise spontaneously. Thus, there may be a need for the state to intervene for the sake of improving the general good. This is one basic motivation for government intervention. Throughout history, however, state interventions have come to replace much that could have worked well as voluntary transactions. And the results of state interventions have, to a large extent, not been beneficial for the public good—quite the contrary.[313]

Public choice research provides explanations for this. The stakeholders of the political arena—voters, politicians, civil servants—will pursue their self-interest. But contrary to the market, this will be a zero-sum battle that does not benefit the general good of society. A voter might

[313] Tullock (2006).

strongly desire a certain benefit from the state in one area, say agri-cultural subsidies to his or her farm. He or she will assume that other tax-payers will accept the bill for the subsidies in exchange for the farmer agreeing to pay for things desired by other groups, such as unemployment benefits, state child-care benefits or higher pensions. This behaviour, leading to redistribution via the state, is sometimes referred to as rent-seeking. The sum of all the special desires will be massive state interventions in society. The scope for voluntary trans-actions in the plus-sum arena decreases. This damages the general good, not least since it harms dynamism and innovation and reduces economic growth.[314]

Many politicians act similarly, which has been described as "logrolling". A politician is usually focused on one or a few issues, most likely those of importance to his or her constituencies. In exchange for support from other politicians for the issue of impor-tance, he or she will support a large number of other issues important to colleagues. A UK Member of Parliament said: *I attend committee meetings and vote on things I don't care about at all in order to get the people who are really interested in those subjects to attend my meeting. And then I hold up their hands when it comes to a vote.*[315] Though prob-ably exaggerating at the end, clearly he pursued his self-interest and exchanged his support for that of his colleagues. There might be agri-culture subsidies in exchange for higher unemployment benefits—without regard to the common good.

Politicians' interest in specific issues rather than the general good is often obvious, from campaign posters to voting in parliament. When you meet Members of Parliament, you may find they introduce

---

[314] Murphy, Shleifer & Vishny (1993).

[315] Tullock (2006).

themselves not by mentioning their party affiliation but from which constituency they come or which committee—traffic, health or agriculture—they belong to. Thus, they largely work together with politicians from other parties in their constituencies against other constituencies, or with politicians in their committee against the interests of other committees. The sum of all these specific issues and political self-interests might very well not benefit the general interest of society. In fact, it is quite unlikely that it does. The result will be more state interventions.

When many citizens pay for a large benefit for a small group, the cost for each tax-payer is limited. This is the argument and mechanism when politicians try to obtain certain favours for their constituency or special group. But when one group gets a privilege from the state, there will be a slippery slope that makes it possible for other groups to make justified demands for similar treatment. And when the cost of paying for favours to everyone instead of a few is to be paid, the sum of the bill is not low anymore. State interventions increase and taxes rise, which has undeniably happened. And the negative effects of every single privilege on society as a whole are easily seen: Employment protection for those that have jobs makes a larger number of others unemployed. Protecting existing taxi drivers raises the price for a taxi trip and increases waiting time. Regulating product markets, protecting some producers, will decrease entrepreneurship and hamper the creation of new products and jobs. Subsidising agriculture leads to higher prices for the consumer and fewer export opportunities for poor countries.

In 1983, the Social Democratic government in Sweden introduced a system known as "Wage Earner Funds". A certain tax on corporate profits was introduced, and the revenue was transferred to the collective funds, with trade union members of the boards. The first idea was that the funds would increase their ownership in the private corporations and, with time, be very influential or even gain a majority. The actual Funds introduced in 1983 were much more limited. This policy was a huge concession to the main trade union, and the ministers of that government subsequently admitted that they had been secretly against the funds, knowing very well that they would harm society as a whole. Indeed, since the Funds were abolished by a centre-right government in 1991, the Social Democrats have never made a similar proposal again. The finance minister, Kjell-Olof Feldt, was caught by a camera with a telephoto lens during the main debate about the Funds in Parliament, writing a rather revealing note on a bit of paper:

"Wage earner funds are a damned shit
But now we have dragged them all the way here
Then they will be filled with every bigwig
Who has supported us in our struggle
Now we don't need to go any more rounds
Before Sweden is filled with funds."[316]

This "rent-seeking society" also changes the incentives. It becomes less important for people to pursue any productive activity—innovating, investing, working—and more important to lobby for privileges from the state.[317] If a large share—perhaps a majority—of the population of a country is to an extent dependent on support from the state, the rent-seeking has reached a very high level. Every group with a benefit will resist the specific reductions for that group, since the reductions for them will be substantial and the gains for the whole of society will be more diffuse. Just as the "market failure" of

---

[316] *Stockholms-Tidningen* (1983).

[317] Krueger (1974).

the polluters—where nobody had the incentive to voluntarily act—motivated state interventions, this "politics failure" creates a situation where all groups block changes that would benefit all.

Civil servants—or bureaucrats, to use the traditional term—allegedly work for the state pursuing aims decided by politicians for the cause of the public good. To a large extent, however, individual civil servants will work for their self-interest too. And their main self-interest is to expand the bureaucracy. At the end of the year, they will spend whatever they have left in the budget so that it will not be smaller next year. In fact, they have an incentive to spend more than they have, so they can expand in coming years. They will engage in efforts to show their political bosses the increasing need of their work in the future—and may engage in communication with the public to underline the need for their services. Quite frequently, for example, public food authorities send alarms about the possibility of poisonous food appearing in stores, if the authorities are not given more resources. Another example might be public unemployment agencies being inefficient in finding jobs—for the simple reason that if unemployment decreases, there will be a more limited need for their services. There is an inherent driving force in all administrations to grow—in size, budget, power, influence and importance. And they will resist any development in the opposite direction.[318]

Game theories can provide explanations for policy outcomes. The current situation can be described as "political equilibrium". In a co-operative game theory model, reforms would be the result of "bargaining between interest groups and the government". The purpose of a model is of course to isolate certain parts of the very complex realities. In reality, there are of course many other actors, mecha-

---

[318] Tullock (2006).

nisms and methods. Thus, models reflect simplified bits of reality, not the whole picture. But one element of policymaking and gaining support for it undoubtedly concerns bargaining between politicians and interest-groups. And the actions by interest-groups are very relevant for the prospects for reform. The bargaining process that leads to a policy outcome might not lead to an efficient economic result. Interest-groups may have formed coalitions to pursue their joint compromise towards the government, which might benefit them, but not society as a whole. This outcome might also remain very persistent over time, because of the broad support among the interest groups, despite the inefficiency for society as a whole.[319] The equilibrium might however be changed, by other special interests being added or some changing position—and suddenly, the special interest consensus is gone and the policies are likely to change.

What the state will be doing—which policies that politicians pursue— is thus a consequence of a number of factors, not just the direct preferences of voters. The mechanisms described can explain the growth of state interventions—despite them sometimes being outright harmful for society as a whole—as well as the difficulties in reducing, abolishing or altering existing interventions. There will be resistance from the systems themselves. In the field of "political economy", such factors are analysed in order to explain policies in different areas. A study of the determinants of government size, for example, identified several important factors: "The size of government and the structure of taxation jointly depend on the traditional demand for publicly provided goods, coercion exercised under majority rule, the supply of taxable activities and the distribution of political influence, as well as on the nature of the legislative and other institutions."[320]

---

[319] Sánches-Mier (2005).

[320] Tridimas & Winer (2005).

Just as these factors might explain current institutions and policies, they may explain change in society. If one or two major factors change, there will be a change in policy. There are factors within and outside political control, but when some of them change, the outcome for society will be affected by their interaction. A study about such "social pacts" in Europe concluded:

"We are witnessing a period of transition in which the market is clearly more important than in the past and in which international constraints and influences have increased. ...a combination of strong external pressures and internal demand for policy innovation may lead from experimentation with new organisational forms to their consolidation."[321]

Much attention has been devoted to analysing the labour market institutions from the perspective of political economy. Why have labour markets often proven difficult to liberalise despite high unemployment and well established positive results from reforms in other countries? The insider-outsider theory has provided a framework, where the insiders are people with jobs and outsiders are the unemployed. Policies are often designed to protect the interests of the insiders, not least since their organisations tend to be very influential in several countries. They also tend to resist reforms that decrease their employment protection despite that leading to more outsiders getting a job. The protection of insiders may take forms like minimum wages and employment protection.[322]

However, there are also forces that operate in the opposite direction. Unemployment in itself creates some pressure for reform, also because it makes insiders more likely to be unemployed one day,

---

[321] Rhodes (2001).

[322] Lindbeck & Snower (2002).

which would change their preferences towards liberalisation.[323] Evidence suggests that it may prove difficult to get enough political support for a complete liberalisation of the labour market, but partial liberalisations may be possible. Such two-tier systems—where groups are exempted from rigid regulation—can lead to support for more flexibility in the entire labour market later.[324]

Ideas

Politicians do not create policy ideas by themselves. They may formulate policies and advocate them, but they do not come up with the ideas—others do. Alain Madelin, former finance minister of France, has said that "politicians are consumers of ideas, not producers".[325] This does not diminish the role of politicians; it is enough to have the tasks of formulating a policy, gaining support for it, manoeuvring through decision-making process and implementing it. But others perform the analyses that lead to ideas and eventually reform proposals. Usually, the idea is shaped in the academic rationality rather than the political. But correctly packaged, it may reach the political agenda. There may be a need for change in some area but not enough to lead to political action. Several distinctive steps can be identified in a process from idea to political action. First, someone must identify the issue. Second, the issue must reach the political agenda. Third, there must be analysis of the causes of a perceived problem. Fourth, solutions should be proposed.

So, where do ideas come from? And how do they get onto the political agenda? Can the climate of ideas be affected by politicians? The

[323] Saint-Paul, Bean & Bertola (1996).
[324] Saint-Paul (1993).
[325] Madelin (2007).

economic development of the West during the 20th century is in itself a study of the origin and influence of ideas. In the early 20th century, economies were characterised by limited state intervention. Then came the stock market crash of 1929, which many analysts interpreted as evidence of the market economy's inherent instability. It was sometimes even seen as evidence that Karl Marx was right in claiming that capitalism would eventually collapse. Ideas arguing that the state had to do intervene extensively in the economy—to have a leading role in economic development and avoid recessions— gained ground. The main person shaping these ideas was the econo- mist John Maynard Keynes. The economic and academic ideas trans- formed into policies throughout the Western world, further devel- oped by a number of scholars and civil servants. In the United States, Franklin D Roosevelt launched his New Deal which featured numer- ous interventions by new public authorities. As late as in the early 1970s, President Richard Nixon said that "we're all Keynesians now" as he launched price controls.

In Western Europe, the new economic ideas went further than in the US, with the state's grip on the economy becoming very tight. The starting point after 1945 was widespread misery in countries devas- tated by war, and the question was which economic system would deliver reconstruction and prosperity the best. Many were haunted by memories of the crises in the 1930s, blamed on *laissez-faire* eco- nomics, and the policies launched went in the opposite direction. Taxes, regulations and public services grew rapidly. Companies were nationalised. The state borrowed and spent in economic downturns to avoid recessions and aimed at doing the opposite in good times (which did not happen). Large budget deficits, rising public debt and inflation followed. European countries introduced what was referred to as a "mixed economy": that is, a mix of centrally planned and mar- ket economy.

An influential report proposing vast state intervention was written by William Beveridge and its conclusions spread to many countries. The socialist Fabian Society, with its famous members, exerted great influence in the UK. French President Charles de Gaulle explained that the state must hold on to the "levers of command" and France introduced economic planning—*planification.* West Germany stuck largely to the market economy, adding the prefix "social" to it. Finance minister Ludwig Erhard was the main defender of this order. But strong forces worked for more state intervention and the election in 1949 stood, in the words of Chancellor Konrad Adenauer, between "social market economy" and "centrally planned economy", with the former winning very narrowly. Many eyes were turned to the East, where the Soviet Union seemed to have a very efficient economy. The Soviets even had the upper hand in the race to space, with the Sputnik satellite being launched in 1957.[326]

Friedrich Hayek wrote "The Road to Serfdom" back in 1944, arguing that the centrally planned economy can never work and that it would lead to political dictatorship.[327] Although it became a best-seller, it did not affect the trend towards more centrally planned economy in the decades to come. But starting in the 1970s, the train of events did eventually turn round. The decisive moment came in the UK in the late 1970s, where people such as Hayek, Keith Joseph, Ralph Harris and Anthony Fischer formulated a new economic agenda. They founded the Institute of Economic Affairs and Centre for Policy Studies, which co-operated closely with politicians such as Margaret Thatcher. Their critique of central planning coincided with massive economic problems in the UK stemming from ever greater

---

[326] Yergin & Stanislaw (1998).

[327] Hayek (1994).

state intervention. Their new agenda for a freer economy of competition and entrepreneurship became a force in the public debate.

These ideas became what is today referred to as Thatcherism and they provided the foundation for the political agenda that reversed the UK economic development and fundamentally changed the political landscape there and abroad.[328] During the 1980s and 1990s, most developed countries reformed in the same direction. In the United States, a number of institutes were founded and expanded during the decades to come. National economists, institutes and think-tanks like the IEA played important roles as countries turned around. Today, Europe has at least 130 market-oriented think-tanks that play important roles in shaping ideas, participating in debate and influencing politicians.[329] There are also numerous other independent institutes and non-governmental organisations arguing their case—in different fields and with different methods.

Ideas are shaped by independent thinking and analysis. This may take place in universities, which underlines the importance of a high degree of independence of education and research from the state and the current political order. The group of private institutes or think-tanks is diverse, but the most successful ones manage to combine research and economics with an understanding of politics, thus being able to make the ideas politically relevant. Strong ideas, like those of Keynes in his time and of Hayek later, will have an impact on the leaders of society and the debate and in the end influence politics too. Pursuing new ideas, breaking new ground, opening up

---

[328] Blundell (2005).

[329] The Stockholm Network, based in London, has most of these think-tanks as members; see The Stockholm Network (2007). Of course there are institutes with other, and opposing, views and ideas as well, but their number seems not to be publicly gathered or revealed.

new perspectives—in the intellectual as well as the broader debate—are tasks that independent thinkers may perform. State-funded agencies with a degree of independence, such as councils and committees, can sometimes also play similar roles, though being closer to the current political leadership and the established ideas. There is always a risk that the tasks of state-funded institutes mainly concern providing academic arguments for established policies. Politicians need new ideas, even if those ideas challenge the ones they currently believe in, and there is a need to have an open and vibrant society with independent analysts and scholars.[330]

The intellectual debate is important for policy ideas, but a number of other factors can contribute to long-lasting substantial political change in a society and also which framework of values and norms will dominate. It is one thing to provide policy solutions to current problems or to lobby politicians for short-term change, but a totally different matter to change society and alter the agenda. In the latter case, success is not about changing a policy proposal but affecting which policy proposals will be launched in the future. A change in the climate of ideas, in other words. This is what happened with both Keynesianism and Thatcherism. No political party or movement has ever been successful in terms of achieving change in society without adopting and developing a long-term policy programme based on firmly founded ideas. Lord Maurice Saatchi, former chairman of the UK Conservative party, claimed this was the main explanation for the election defeat in 2005. "If you don't stand for something, you will fall for anything."[331]

---

[330] An extensive account of independent economic thinking on theory and policy, its conditions and its subsequent policy effects, is found in Skousen (2001).

[331] Saatchi (2005).

The US conservative movement has also been successful in recent decades. Regardless of which political party has the presidency or dominates Congress, America is a much more conservative society than almost any European country. The Democrats, though many of them oppose conservative policies, have adapted to that climate. Bill Clinton, after all, declared "the end of big government". The ordinary American wants lower taxes, freer enterprise, more traditional values and less gun control than the ordinary German, Frenchman, Swede or Slovak. This is a consequence of a forceful conservative movement working for decades, with think-tanks, grassroots organisations, talk radio and skilful leaders. Beatrice Webb, one of the founders of the UK's socialist Fabian Society claimed: "There is no such thing as a spontaneous public opinion. It all has to be manufactured from a centre of conviction and energy". Of course people have a will of their own and unpredicted events take place all the time, but major and lasting changes are often the result of long and dedicated work by strongly engaged people.[332]

Organisations

In an increasingly globalised and interdependent world, international organisations of course also have important roles in policymaking. Non-governmental organisations, such as humanitarian, environmental and anti-globalisation movements, clearly have an impact on the debate and ultimately on the political agenda. The rise of the Attac movement in the early 2000s led French President Jacques Chirac to propose a form of Tobin tax on global transactions and Swedish Prime Minister Göran Persson to quote Lenin to try to appease the

---

[332] A recent and detailed historic account of the American Conservative movement is found in Micklethwait & Woolridge (2005).

Attac activists.[333] The Attac movement was factually wrong on most accounts but was energetic, had many members and attracted much media attention, which is what got the political machinery going.[334]

Intergovernmental organisations such as the OECD, IMF and the World Bank also have policy implications for member countries. They provide research, country comparisons and policy advice. Though member governments put restraints on its intellectual freedom and external communication, governments may happily "delegate" the task of providing arguments for change. There may be incentives for member governments to come out well in country comparisons and they might feel certain obligations to at least react to the recommendations. Several intergovernmental multilateral organisations also have direct policy roles for countries in crisis, especially the IMF and the World Bank. As lenders, they impose policy demands on the recipients.

One international organisation has more powers than any other: the European Union. It is not only an intergovernmental organisation but also has sovereignty over certain policy areas, such as trade and agriculture, for the 27 member countries. The EU shapes and implements policies by law, directives and recommendations in member countries. It has been estimated that in some policy areas, a majority of new regulations in European countries today come from the European Union. Initiatives come from the non-elected EU Commission and decisions are taken, sometimes by a qualified majority, in the Council of Ministers from the member states and the European Parliament with directly elected members. Many advisory committees

---

[333] *The Economist* (2005a), *Daily Telegraph* (2001).

[334] The most thorough account of all the points where the Attac movement—and similar movements—were wrong in their analyses of the world economy as well as in what their proposals would actually lead to can be found in Norberg (2003).

exist too.[335] Much has been written about the EU's impact on Europe and how it will develop and a fierce debate about the EU's future is raging between those who want more powers for the EU and those who want the opposite. On the other scale, the questions concern what the EU should do, to the extent that it should be doing something. This is largely the traditional debate about the extent of state interventions in society—the EU, though international, represents the state—and what form they should have. A parallel debate is how to make the EU work better and be more democratically accountable.

The economic effects of the EU and its policies could, in highly simplified terms, be divided into two categories. The first category is a liberating effect: tearing down borders to trade between member states, creating a single market, stressing sound macroeconomic frameworks, addressing national subsidies, having market economic criteria for EU membership and enhancing institutional competition. That part of the EU has undeniably contributed to reform, growth and employment in European countries. The single market programme was launched in 1992 and a number of studies have analysed the effects so far. Trade has increased more than it would otherwise have done, which has also boosted competition and thus contributed to higher productivity.[336] EU GDP is estimated to be some 2 percentage points higher today than it would have been without the Single Market. Furthermore, it has been estimated to have led to the creation of an additional 2.75 million jobs.[337] Following the liberalisation of energy and telecom markets as part of the Lisbon Agenda consumer

---

[335] A more detailed account of how the European Union and its institutions work can be found in McCormick (2005).

[336] European Commission (2006c).

[337] European Commission (2007).

prices have decreased.[338] The 2004 enlargement process also widened the Single Market, further boosting its effects on trade, investments and growth.[339]

The second category of EU economic effects is the opposite, an interventionist approach: subsidies to agriculture, working time regulations, at times protectionist external trade policies, possible harmonisation of some taxes, and more regulations. Leaders of EU member states often try to introduce policies that benefit their own countries, claiming that it is for Europe as a whole. Sometimes they try to persuade the EU to launch policies that are too difficult to introduce domestically. An initially controversial proposal that will later on be accepted can be blamed on "Brussels". The EU is a traditional political arena—of bargaining, self-interest, rent-seeking, special interests and powerful civil servants. The policy result is always some kind of compromise. It is impossible to tell which of the two economic effects will dominate in the future; it is part of the battle of ideas and policies. What is apparent, however, is that there is no such thing as a purely national political arena anymore—international aspects are integrated. Also, limits on public power and democratic accountability are important for EU political power as well as for national power. That poses new restraints and opportunities for policymakers, described by Tony Blair as his most important lesson from ten years as UK prime minister.[340]

Intergovernmental organisations create political co-operation, international regulations and exchange of views on policies. The global economy has not only increased trade, competition and interdepend-

---

[338] European Commission, DG Energy and Transport,
http://europa.eu/energy/gas/publications/index_en.htm
[339] European Commission (2006d).
[340] Blair (2007).

ence. It has also put restraints on what governments can do without adverse effects, in particular following the liberalisation of financial markets. Countries today that start nationalising companies, raising taxes dramatically and regulating markets (like most governments did during the decades after World War II) would immediately suffer from lower investment, a falling exchange rate, falling stock markets and thus a range of economic problems. Indeed, this happened to France in 1980 when President François Mitterrand introduced such policies. They were quickly reversed.

Despite this, states are far from powerless. Success in large part depends on what governments do, and there are many ways to achieve it. There is indeed a great difference between countries that have taken decisions to reform or not. For all the importance of globalisation and international organisations, ultimately national governments still have the main role in politics. Governance gets its legitimacy from a "demos", a group of people that have enough in common to feel that there are collective decisions for them that are legitimate—and that is still mostly a fact on the national level.[341]

Agenda and Policy Process

There are ideas. And there are politicians. How do they meet? What does the way from academic knowledge to policy proposal look like? First, there must be some reason to act. Then there must be an idea about how to act. Finally, there have to be incentives for politicians to take the final step and stand up for a proposal. The rest is a matter of engaging in the political battle of arguing for the proposal, con-

---

[341] An overview of how international organisations affect nations, governments and politics is in Gilpin (2001).

fronting vested interests and eventually implementing the decision. How something at first becomes an issue that seems to demand political action might intuitively seem simple. If there is a problem and it is in the gift of politicians to do something about it, do they have to? No, some problems become political issues whereas some problems that are perhaps equally serious do not. And when it has become a political issue, surely then it is inevitable that politicians will act? Again no: some issues remain on the agenda for a long time and nothing happens, until perhaps they become more serious. They may also fade away. A reason for inaction might be that there is no policy proposal, no solution. Lastly, even if an issue is considered a problem and there are policy proposals, still nothing may happen. If, from the political perspective, action is judged as too risky or compli-cated, the issue may be neglected until the price of remaining inactive is too high. In the end, there must be political incentives for action.

A traditional model of the policy process described above describes it in stages, preferably with boxes on a line. The policy process starts with the issue emergence, continues with agenda setting, alternative selection, enactment and implementation—and ends with evalua-tion.[342] This model and may be relevant as a framework for the stages but it conveys an image of the process being much more orderly than is the case in reality. In real politics in real countries, the process is more chaotic, fluent and changing, and may quite possibly happen partly in the reverse order. Chaos theory provides conclusions about the nature of how society and politics evolve:

"Randomness, chaos, and non-linear dynamics are important character-istic properties of living systems, of historical process of change and con-tinuity and of evolution, but certainly not the other way around: not the

---

[342] Birkland (2005).

rule of evolution... The key role is played by the self-evolving process of continuity accelerated or decelerated by human intervention in changing the nature, as well as chaotic and accidental events."[343]

Thus, what the people involved in the policy process do will be of great importance. But the development might change simply because the very nature of complex systems is change itself, which is sometimes unpredictable. There may also be a great number of unforeseeable events that can trigger changes. Hence, moving from idea to policy and political action is never an orderly process. In his classic work, Professor John W Kingdon instead identified three "streams" that flow independently but have to converge for change to take place: the streams of problems, policies and politics. When they coincide, the window of opportunity will be open and there are good chances of policy change.[344]

Problems: How do some issues become political issues that may attract the focus of governments and their civil servants? Indicators, focusing events and feedback are three mechanisms that may bring a problem to attention. Various kinds of *indicators* are used to analyse developments in society compared to policy intent and usually take the form of statistics and figures. The indicators may show that there is a problem that deserves attention. The more well-known they are, the more likely it is that there will be attention. *Focusing events* can take various forms, such as disasters, personal experience and symbols. Crises are one kind of focusing event that can bring a problem to attention. *Feedback* may provide evidence that society develops in a different way than intended from a certain policy, and thus there may be a need for change. As problems arise on the agenda they may

---

[343] Farazmand (2003).

[344] Kingdon (2003).

also fade away because a second-best solution has been applied or people get used to the condition.

Policies: How, then, are policies shaped that attempt to solve the current or future problems? In reference to the long-term, broad, historic lines of the influence of ideas, the answer is having an open society with independent thinkers and a vibrant debate. The slightly shorter-term policies, with a focus on single issues, are usually generated, drafted and shaped in widely defined policy communities (that is, governmental experts in planning or budget offices and non-governmental experts working for think-tanks and interest groups). This is an intellectual process that also has to evolve into a proposal which is technically feasible and adapted to constraints such as budgets. The step from having a proposal to the point where more than individual politicians may consider it is a big one, though. It takes years of "softening up" involving extensive and persistent work by "political entrepreneurs" who try to gain support for their proposal. Professor Kingdon reveals a story from one of his respondents, a then-young advisor to a US senator. After one year's work, he had finalised work on a new bill and the senator gladly agreed to present it the day after but refused to read the proposal beforehand, commenting: *"We'll introduce this tomorrow, but it will take 20 to 25 years for it to be brought into being. If it takes that long, there's not much point in my looking at the bill now, is there?"*

Politics: When there is an issue to be solved and a proposal for solving it there must also be political interest in doing so. The political stream flows along its own lines and is affected largely by external developments, such as public opinion, international events and campaigns by interest groups. Internal factors that affect the political stream include shifts of persons in leading positions or a shift of parliamentary majority. Sometimes a policy proposal with politically appealing content might be rejected by politicians just because it comes from what is perceived to be the wrong sources. A left-leaning government may find it hard to adopt a proposal from business organisations, despite actually liking the proposal, because the public connection might create a debate of unholy alliances.[345] But when a proposal is accepted by leading politicians, the process may get under way quickly. Inaction may swiftly be replaced by action. When an issue seems to be moving and the political dynamics work for change, the process often happens rapidly. Many of those that have remained inactive out of fear of taking risks throw themselves into the game, trying to protect their interests and gain influence. The political stream is a complex entity but not entirely unpredictable. Some factors that affect it—such as the general economic development, election dates and developments in comparable countries—can to some extent be predicted.

Sometimes the three streams converge and open a window of opportunity. If action is taken, it increases the probability of change in other areas. "Events spill over to adjacent areas because politicians find there is a reward for riding the same horse that brought benefit before, because the winning coalition can be transferred to other issues, and because one can argue from precedent."[346] Sometimes, policy changes occur quite dramatically, with many and substantial changes after a longer period of stability. Although it is not always easy to spot the incident that triggers the rapid change or the mechanisms involved, the "punctuated equilibrium" theory provides an answer. According to this theory, stability may be underpinned by what is referred to as a policy monopoly, with a closed system of policymaking, perhaps supported by established interests. When an

---

[345] Johnson (2001).

[346] Kingdon (2003).

event takes place that displays some major problem with the current order, the policy monopoly as a whole tends to fall apart, unleashing a number of changes. This may also happen if the balance of supporting interests changes, by one supporter disappearing or a new one entering the game.[347]

Public Opinion and the Media

Representative government today no longer takes the form of classical parliamentarianism or traditional party democracy but can rather be called an "audience democracy". Elections are more personalised, experts in political communication abound, public opinion is central to policymaking and politics, and the political debate has been transferred from parliament or party to the public arena. Policies are shaped in public debate and politicians use public opinion in pursuing proposals. Political communication and mobilisation are central parts of governing. This can be seen as a process of building an agenda, where the political actors, the media and the citizens interact.[348] The mass media—the more traditional printed press or radio as well as TV and Internet—play an important role as a channel of communication and as an actor itself in the public debate. This is where reform ideas may emerge, their support is tested and effects are debated. It is the public debate and its main features and actors that constitute most of the reform landscape, and it will affect whether policies ever become politics.

The actors that participate in the public debate may be divided into three categories: decision-makers from different arenas, the media

---

[347] True, Jones & Baumgartner (1999).

[348] Kriesi, Hanspeter in Esser & Pfetsch, eds (2004).

and the independent challengers, such as interest groups or think-tanks. They may pursue different strategies in attempting to put their ideas on the public agenda and then win public support for them. The *decision-makers* may choose to "go public" with a proposal to win broader public support, which makes winning the political game much easier in the end. This can be preceded by measures to analyse public opinion and adapt the proposal, such as focus groups or opinion polls. In its proactive version, this strategy is about initiating and leading public opinion rather than following opinions initiated by others. By going public before making the political manoeuvres, however, decision-makers lock their position on the issue, making bargaining more difficult. The *independent challengers* that ultimately want to influence policies by setting the public agenda may use different strategies to succeed. There may be protest politics—mobilising support for protest actions—or information politics—presenting credible information and ideas to specific target groups at well-defined points in time. These efforts are largely directed towards getting the message across via the media.[349]

The media are the crucial channel for communication in the public debate but they are an actor in the political process too. In a classic expression, the media deals with "the world outside and the pictures in our heads".[350] Our perceptions of the world, how it works, politics, proposals and events are largely shaped by the media and they may set the agenda for the public debate.[351] First, they determine whether they will actually report on issues, proposals or actions at all. By sometimes focusing on issues that decision-makers do not want to become public they fulfil a controlling function in society. Second,

---

[349] Kriesi, Hanspeter in Esser & Pfetsch, eds (2004).

[350] The quote is the title of the opening chapter of Walter Lippmann's Public Opinion, 1922.

[351] McCombs (2004).

the media also structure reality for citizens and orientate us, as well as evaluating policies and initiating policy debates by focusing on failures or highlighting problems in society. Frequently, the media use opinion polls and present them as news, which will influence politicians' agendas. In modern society, governing needs day-to-day support from citizens to be forceful and proactive, not just the support of a majority in elections. The media prefer to report on dramatic events or developments and more personalised issues and thus tend to dramatise and personalise reality. They also report less about issues and more about the political game itself.[352]

How the world is described—including economics, politics and proposals—will be influenced by the journalist's personal view of the world. A survey showed that in Germany and Italy, more than 70 per cent of journalists that responded consider it very or quite important in their work to "champion values and ideas". In the US, the UK and Sweden, more than 40 per cent of journalist respondents said they considered it very or quite important to "influence politics". The results of another survey showed that journalists in Western democracies identify more with the political left than with the political right.[353]

Though there are several common features between the news media in different countries in the Western world—and media trends that spread from country to country—there are differences too. One study distinguishes between three models of media systems, which is partly a consequence of the interrelation between the media and political cultures and structures. The first is the polarised pluralist model, found around the Mediterranean and characterised by extensive

---

[352] Johnson (2001).

[353] Patterson & Donsbach in Esser & Pfetsch, eds (2004).

state intervention in society, a high degree of ideological polarisation
and a general view of the media as champions of different views and
ideologies. The second is the democratic corporatist model, found in
Central and Northern Europe. It features a strong role for established
special interests and the media characterised by an advocacy culture.
The third is the liberal model of the North Atlantic, where representation in society is more individualistic, special interests are regarded
with scepticism and the media is seen as an information provider
and watchdog of government.[354]

Opinion polls are one way to find information about the current
views of people on different matters. They should be interpreted
with caution, since views may change and we sometimes hold con-
flicting views and it is difficult to know the priorities of single views.
Some international opinion polls are conducted regularly and may
show regional variations and changes in views over time. At times,
they deal with topics of relevance for reform. In the 2006 Eurobarometer, 64 per cent of respondents from across the EU said free competition was the best guarantee of economic prosperity and 62 per cent
agreed that the state intervenes too much in their lives.[355] Another
Europe-wide opinion poll, in March 2007, showed massive support
in all the 27 EU countries (except Finland, where the opinion is 50:50)
for the view that taxes have to be reduced for Europe to be able to
compete in today's world, though there is also broad support for
"protection" against international competition.[356]

The Pew Research Centre conducted an opinion poll of the views
among people aged 18–25 versus the views of people aged 26–40 in

---

[354] Hallin & Mancini (2004).

[355] European Commission, Eurobarometer 66—Public Opinion in the European Union,
December 2006.

[356] Open Europe (2007).

the US. The young—called Generation Next—are more positive to immigration, globalisation, companies and generally more tolerant, though also more tolerant towards state intervention.[357] Though public opinion may shift—and there is much to suggest that there will always be initial resistance to change—some values, particularly among the young, would clearly support the direction of many reforms. But there are also results that might confirm the thesis of voters generally leaning towards positions against trade and markets.

The actors in the public debate all interrelate with each other and will react in several steps to the strategies of the others. The outcome will have an impact on whether ideas and policies ever become politics. Decision-makers have substantial opportunities to influence the media since they possess knowledge, communication experts and actually provide material for today's news broadcasts or tomorrow's articles by journalists. Adapting to the news logic and storytelling, they work in the opposite way to academic endeavours, starting with the conclusion and ending with the background. This enables them to access the media on the media's terms. Even on occasions when the media sets the agenda, there will be opportunities for deci-sion-makers to get a message through to the audience. Spin-doctors, as political media advisors are sometimes called, may be highly effi-cient but their role is limited to getting the message across or reac-tively handling issues that emerge. Their work cannot replace political content. There must be a bottom line—policy content—for public opinion to move forward.

A reformer has to act in the landscape of public opinion. This part of the reform landscape is not necessarily for or against particular reform proposals but more a matter of packaging, message and strategy. For

---

[357] The Pew Research Centre (2007a).

politicians, it may be useful if independent actors do the ground-work of introducing and arguing for proposals. But there are ways of setting the agenda, mobilising public opinion and successfully handling the media.

Markets and Politics

The need for reform is usually described in rational, economic terms and the analysis is academic. Many economists and businessmen who see a need for reform understand the market and its rationality. From that perspective, it seems odd that politicians do not act and undertake reform to a much larger extent. That is what companies that compete in a market do all the time. But, as shown, politicians do not start with the academic, rational, market perspective and add a slight touch of blurry political reasons to it. They act according to the rules of their arena. A comparison between the market arena and the political arena can both provide insights into politics from those used to the market and further describe the features of politics.[358]

In a democracy, the state has a monopoly on the use of force (except in self-defence, when it is normally allowed for citizens too). This is one of the fundamental characteristics of a state. Thus, every time the state intervenes in society its action is backed up by its monopoly on the use of force. The two main questions for politicians are *how much* the state should do, that is, how many and how large its interven-

---

[358] Political science professor Deborah Stone's book "Policy Paradox" is a thorough and detailed account of the rationality of the political arena, with numerous empirical examples. She also frequently compares politics and markets. Sometimes, she reveals personal views on policy matters—which are clearly not in favour of conservative policies—and that may be reflected in some of the conclusions, for example about the effects of government interventions. To an extent, the comparison above is based on her account. Stone (2002).

TABLE 5. MARKETS AND POLITICS — VENUS AND MARS

Market	Politics
Individual decisions, free exchange	Collective decisions founded on monopoly of force
Plus-sum game	Zero-sum game
Consumers, self-interest	Citizens, collective decisions, self-interest, "public interest"
Influence on consumers	Influence in all directions
Competition	Co-operation, loyalty and competition
Individuals	Individuals, groups and organisations
Accurate and complete information	Ambiguous, interpretive, incomplete, strategically manipulated information
Free exchange, demand	Ideas, persuasion, pursuit of power
Clearly stated goals	Ambiguously stated goals
Imagining as many alternatives as possible	Politically relevant selection of alternatives
Each alternative clearly defined	Blended alternatives, one-sided arguments
Costs and benefits of each alternative openly evaluated	Presenting the consequences that will make your alternative look the best
Choosing the alternative that will maximise total welfare	Choosing the alternative that will benefit important constituencies but portray it as best for general welfare

tions in society should be, and to the extent that it should do something, *what* should it do? Politics revolves around these issues and it is a battle about having the power to run the state. Every time politicians decide that the state should intervene, that intervention replaces a possible exchange in the market.

Contrary to voluntary exchange between individuals in a market, which is a plus-sum game where participants win (or else the exchange would not take place), politics is a zero-sum game. There are only 100 per cent votes in an election and a fixed number of seats in parliament, so if one wins, another will lose. There may be several political arenas, such as a second parliamentary chamber or regional assemblies, but each single political arena is a zero-sum game. This fact has major effects on the nature of politics since it is largely a battle to gain and keep political power. A company in the market will be successful if it develops better and more value-for-money products that consumers demand. Objective criteria exist to define its success, such as sales and profits. Politicians try to satisfy their consumers—the voters—but the political market is different. Innovation is not always beneficial and the criteria for success are subjective and changing.

The bottom line of politics is running the state, which provides rights for and places demands on its citizens. The justification for collective decisions is that they are in the interest of all citizens, that is, the public interest. Even if decisions benefit only a few they will always be justified with the public interest. A political decision often comes into conflict with the interests of a minority, which is why constitutions, courts of justice and other arrangements put limits on majority rule. But the minority may be bulldozed.[359]

In the market, there are no decisions on behalf of everyone and an actor will only do something if he or she voluntarily wants to do it. A decision can be openly motivated by self-interest since it will not be collectively imposed on someone else. Furthermore, in the market the pursuit of self-interest sometimes involves risk-taking when

---

[359] See a number of typical cases in Shattered Dreams: One Hundred Cases of Government Abuse, National Center for Public Policy Research (2007).

creating and innovating. But when politicians pursue their self-interest—to gain future positions and power—they usually turn rather risk-averse. This is especially true if future personal benefits, such as pensions, are dependent on them being in office for a long time.

In a market, free competition is the mechanism of settling different interests and conflicts between the stakeholders. Conflicts in politics often concern what is perceived to be in the collective interest and what is in an individual's interest: should the citizen be required to pay more tax to public health care, or pay less tax to public health care, in order to keep more money and be able to purchase private health insurance? There are also conflicts about what may be in the interests of different individuals or groups of individuals. Politics is largely about peacefully handling different and legitimate views about society. Single situations may be far from clear-cut and pose intellectual dilemmas. Since political decisions will affect people's lives, often in fundamental ways, numerous and intense attempts will be made to exert influence. In the market, many attempts are made to influence the choices of consumers, for example by commercials. But their degree, form, purpose and reason are different.

In the market, the rule is competition. If there are few barriers to entrepreneurship, trade, investment, consumer choice and work, competition is the automatic result. In politics, there is zero-sum competition. But winning in the zero-sum game—and retaining a high degree of influence between elections—also requires co-operation, not least with stakeholders outside the political arena. It takes forms like coalitions, alliances, movements and networks. Loyalty is essential: there are "friends" and "enemies". And loyalty in politics takes forms like favours, support and future obligations. Bargaining or "logrolling" is commonly used to achieve results.

Lack of future co-operation and loyalty is why politicians become "lame ducks" long before they resign, despite being just as energetic as before and using the same arguments. They can no longer pay back in future favours because they will soon be out of the picture. Covering a European Union summit of heads of government in June 2007, which Tony Blair attended despite having announced his imminent resignation as prime minister, The Economist wrote: "'Why would anyone do Mr Blair a favour at his last summit,' asks one diplomat. 'How is he going to pay them back—in his memoirs?'"[360]

Markets have groups of consumers and different segments. But these are usually temporary and it is ultimately the individual who decides what to do. In politics, groups are something different and longer-lasting and they may organise special interests. Groups are important because most voters belong to several of them and because they become something larger than the sum of their parts in terms of political influence. They can influence the whole political arena in ways that groups could never run an entire market. They may be trade unions, business organisations, farmers associations, student groups, religious groups or human rights organisations. In a corporatist society, they are active participants in the public decision-making process and may be granted semi-public powers, such as trade unions taking care of mandatory unemployment benefit schemes. The opposite model is a more pluralist society, where groups and organisations (except political parties) are not part of public decision-making but instead try to exert influence by means of opinion-forming and lobbying.[361]

Politics is mainly about seeking influence and power. A primary method for achieving it is to use the means of persuasion. A politician

---

[360] *The Economist* (2007e).

[361] Dahl (1989).

will do, write or say that which will persuade the target group. This is why the economically it is not always the most important arguments that are used but rather those that work. Politicians are not trying to persuade economists but people who see other aspects as more important than the academically well-founded ones. The main effect of a proposal might be an increase in foreign trade, but since fewer care about trade than about jobs politicians will say that it is about creating more jobs, though the job effect may factually be more uncertain or smaller. Indeed, this is why politicians may do things that are symbolically valuable, but with very limited real effects. The measure of success is what brings more support, and this may definitely include concrete results but also more besides. It also means that in politics, contrary to the market, many resources in the battle are not scarce. Persuasion is unlimited and in fact increases the more it is successfully used, especially with more people involved.

In terms of identifying alternatives, prioritising and pursuing a goal, politics again differs from the market. Politics is not about identifying all possible alternatives, openly analysing the cases for and against or acknowledging advantages and disadvantages. Politicians do not have sufficient time to gain top-level knowledge about every single issue in front of them before committing themselves to a decision. There are too many issues to deal with, the speed is too high and it might not be in their interest to start with. This has been referred to as "bounded rationality". Second, the process itself does often not start in a rational analysis of the issue and alternatives but at the other end, namely what will be the politically most beneficial proposal? The policy decision is also largely based on earlier standpoints and evolves incrementally.[362] Neither will politicians benefit from stating the advantages and disadvantages openly. They only

---

[362] Birkland (2005).

have a brief time in which to explain why they do something and thus have to focus solely on the advantages. Since their opponents will point to the disadvantages, they do not have to waste their own short time mentioning them. "Admitting" disadvantages may come back to haunt you as you attempt to pursue your policy.

In choosing an alternative among possible policies, a politician has an incentive to make a choice that benefits important constituencies for him or her. This is perfectly natural. Even for politicians there are only 24 hours in a day, so they have to prioritise and will make choices that benefit their future political power. President George W Bush talked a lot about the need for free trade but introduced tariffs on steel because of the perceived needs of a special constituency. Analyses have provided evidence that American society as a whole lost due to this, with 45,000 to 75,000 jobs lost in the industries dependent on steel imports, which employ roughly 40 times as many as the protected steel producers.[363] In the end, American steel producers lost too, since tariffs are artificial protection from competition and simply make industry less competitive. But what is important is sometimes not the accurate information, but what the politician thinks the constituency believes.

Again, some might say that this confirms that politics is a dirty business. And there is a difference between the fine words at the end and the actual political battle beforehand. The 19th century German Chancellor Otto von Bismarck once remarked that people would sleep better at night if they avoided watching the making of laws and sausages alike.[364] It has been said for ages that politics should change

---

[363] Drazen (2004).
[364] More insightful, amusing and slightly cynical quotes about politics by the Iron Chancellor can be found at
www.brainyquote.com/quotes/authors/o/otto_von_bismarck.html

and should be less of a battle, less about tactics, have fewer half-truths and be less focused on criticising opponents. It does not change because these features are the nature of politics. The political arena can improve, by being more transparent, attracting competent people and having better skilled scrutinisers, but a number of basic features will not change. Human nature, the nature of collective action, the nature of the state and the nature of society together create this political arena and reform landscape.

For politicians, this picture is not new but a simple fact of everyday life. Politicians may often seem to wonder why they have to listen to economists and businessmen with their rational but politically irrelevant or impossible arguments. The analyses and arguments of Venus simply do not work on Mars. Does this difference between the market and politics mean that market-oriented policies are by definition unnatural in politics? Partly, perhaps, but not necessarily. It is possible to make the political system work for reform. Economists, business people and academics do not use arguments that are relevant for politicians. It is not enough that a proposal would without doubt lead to higher living standards if it were to create political problems. A reform has to bring political benefits, too. These can be of many different kinds, such as re-election, recognition, positive attention or support from new groups. If such conditions are present then there will be political momentum in favour of reform.

The fact that military metaphors are often used in politics may provide additional information about the nature of politics. It is not just the frequent words like battle, fighting, mobilisation, fronts, ammunition, duel, tactics, army, enemy, attack and artillery. There are also real similarities between politics and war—from a politician's perspective. Carl von Clausewitz famously claimed that war is the continuation of politics by other means.[365] This is not to say that politics should be violent. Quite the opposite, when politics fail violence sometimes erupts, demonstrating the importance of effective political institutions. Politics and war both concern struggles between opposing wills, arouse deep passions and require elaborate strategies and tactics.

Many politicians engaged in the peaceful battle of political power have learned from military strategy. Political success demands mobilisation of supporters, leadership towards a goal, fighting an opponent, co-ordinating many efforts, managing logistics and deploying intelligence, deception and demoralisation.[366] Politicians may be assumed to have their eyes turned on society, but in fact they are focused on how to beat the opponent using every means possible and acceptable. For proposed reforms to be politically relevant they have to be useful ammunition in the political battle and not likely to blow up in your own face.

Summary and Conclusions

Most of us fear losses and we do not take risks. As voters, we lack knowledge about many parts of society and we have a number of misconceptions. Hence, voters will invariably have an initial resistance to change. Politicians have an incentive to work for their constituencies rather than society as a whole, leading to harmful outcomes. Voters who do not know what is best for society may therefore support politicians who actively pursue policies that benefit certain groups rather than all of society. Special interests and groups will try to

[365] von Clausewitz (1984).

[366] Pitney (2000).

glean favours from the state and fight to keep existing privileges. They will claim that reforms harm the public good, but they are merely fighting for their own benefits. Civil servants work to expand their scope and influence. Institutions and policies that harm society as a whole may remain in place for a long time. These features of the political arena are all capable of putting up obstacles to reform and must be considered. Policies, systems and institutions have an inherent desire to grow and resist change—especially reductions of any kind.

Politicians usually do not come up with policy ideas; others do. It is important to have a society with many independent institutes and voices and a free debate. Ideas that make the leap from academic thinking to policy debate and politics can have massive long-term influence. Public committees can also play a role. Non-governmental organisations have an impact on the political direction. Intergovernmental organisations provide comparisons and policy advice, and together with increased interdependence have put restraints on national policies. But national governments still decide the fate of their countries. It is a complex path from idea to policy to political agenda to decision and to implementation. The issue has to become politically relevant, a policy must be shaped, and this proposal must join a favourable political stream. Then, it is up to politicians to propose and defend the policy and manoeuvre in the reform landscape, among other things negotiating the media. Public opinion is a very influential factor in today's politics and the media is both the most important channel of communication and an actor in the public debate. Finally, the political arena is very different from the marketplace. Politics is a zero-sum game, decisions are collective, loyalty is central, co-operation dominates, communication is ambiguous and evaluation is subjective.

HOW TO DO IT

"The essence of a good government is that it is prepared to take difficult decisions necessary to get the long-term prosperity."

MARGARET THATCHER, FORMER UK PRIME MINISTER, 1990[367]

"The only way to produce reform is to have a strong vision and every step has to be consistent with the vision. In changing the traditional model, politicians have to create new securities for citizens. An efficient labour market is a central part of a new model and work is the greatest part of social policy and new security."

MAURIZIO SACCONI, FORMER ITALIAN MINISTER FOR LABOUR[368]

"Therefore measure in terms of five things, use these assessments to make comparisons, and thus find out what the conditions are. The five things are the way, the weather, the terrain, the leadership and discipline... Leadership is a matter of intelligence, trustworthiness, humaneness, courage and sternness When directives are consistently carried out to edify the populace, the populace accepts."

SUN TZU, CHINESE PHILOSOPHER, 2000 YEARS AGO[369]

DESPITE THE NEED FOR REFORM, a large body of reform proposals and evidence of positive effects from reform, there is an established view that reform is politically difficult or even impossible. True,

---

[367] Thatcher, Margaret, House of Commons, 22nd of April 1990,
www.margaretthatcher.org/speeches/displaydocument.asp?docid=110916
[368] Sacconi, Maurizio, Interview, 8 May 2007.
[369] Sun Tzu (1991).

the political arena and the surrounding reform landscape provide numerous obstacles to change. There will always be an initial resistance to change from special interests blocking improvements for the whole of society—and a fear of change in general and thus politicians trying to exploit that fear. But substantial reform is possible, as quite a number of countries have shown, and there are several lessons about how to do it.

Certainly, reform processes can fail, as has happened in a number of countries. In that context, it is worth remembering that the most certain way to fail is to avoid trying. If a government does not even attempt to reform to solve problems and improve society it will surely fail. Politicians who have done nothing may fail to be re-elected. If they lose an election, not even the proud memory of a positive achievement will be left. General election outcomes always contain elements of uncertainty and the risk of losing is at least as likely if a politician is inactive when in office. Governments which do reform can increase their chances of success by following a number of *reform lessons*. In basic terms, these can be summarised as follows:

1. A country's economic and social success or failure is largely decided by policies, not geography, country size, religion or culture. Large countries can reform just as small countries can. The country's future fate is thus within the power of its citizens and their political leaders to change. OECD countries are similar enough in their economic and political situation to emulate each other's solutions.

2. A substantial amount of evidence exists to underpin the case for reform. In each potential reform area, there are analyses to show the problems and provide advice on solutions. Everyone who is interested has access to information about what to do and why to do it.

3. Reforming has proven possible during the last two to three decades, as different countries show to differing degrees. A number of countries have come a long way. Much still remains to be done, but there is a large amount of analyses, proposals and lessons from countries that went ahead of others.

4. The positive economic and social results of reforms have often proven to be quite astonishing—not instantly but surpassing expectations over time. Growth, employment, incomes, education and health care quality have risen and poverty, unemployment and social exclusion have fallen in reformist countries. This is not least because incentives work and because reforms change the operation of society.

5. Change always finds resistance among voters, special interests, civil servants and political opponents, but reforms that have proven to be controversial when launched have usually gained general acceptance afterwards. When a reformist government is voted out of office its reforms are usually not rolled back by the incoming administration, even though such suggestions are often made prior to an election.

6. Governments politically labelled as left and right alike have managed to launch successful reforms, just as governments labelled as both left and right in the 1960s and 1970s expanded the ambit of state intervention in society. Acknowledging the need for reform and what works is largely about pragmatism.

7. One reform wave has often tended to help set off new reforms, thereby contributing to a virtuous circle of reform. Trade reforms have tended to lead to product market reforms, and reforms in product markets have tended to lead to labour market reforms.[370] High growth rates make labour market deregulation more likely.[371]

---

[370] Höj et al (2006).

[371] Saint-Paul (1998).

8. The most far-reaching reforms have taken place in trade, taxes, macroeconomic frameworks and product markets. But large public systems like pensions, health care, education and social security have been substantially reformed in some countries.

9. Reforms will always encounter resistance from political opponents, civil servants, voters, special interests and sections of the media. But their positions and opinions will change over time and there are ways to handle these forces for a reformer.

10. Lastly, a reform opportunity might be opened by an economic crisis but that is not a prerequisite. Many reforms have been launched and implemented without a general crisis. In fact, reforms in specific labour market areas—such as tax wedges, employment protection and benefit systems—have usually taken place during economic upswings.[372] Also, harmful state interventions have often increased in times of crises.[373]

Contrary to what some people appear to believe, reformist governments have usually been re-elected, at least once. This is of course a simplification. Sometimes, governments have been re-elected but in slightly different compositions. They may have received a smaller share of the votes cast in elections yet been able to remain in office. And when they finally did lose an election, the defeat was often attributed by commentators to various alleged mistakes, not least their attempted reforms. The accuracy of such comments can be questioned, but what is really important is to ask the counterfactual question: what would have happened in the same election if the government had remained inactive and not launched reforms? The political outcome could very well have been worse for the govern-

---

[372] Höj et al (2006).

[373] Higgs, Robert, Crisis and Leviathan, Critical Episodes in the Growth of American Government, Pacific Institute for Public Policy 1987.

ment, and the economic and social outcome for the country would certainly have been.

In the reformist countries described in this book, the governments that came a long way have been re-elected at least once in every case, except in Sweden. *In Ireland, Australia, Slovakia, Estonia, Iceland, Denmark, Spain, the UK, New Zealand, the US, Switzerland and the Netherlands, reformist governments have gained re-election.* France, Germany and Italy were previously mentioned not because they achieved a great deal but to point out that even they made some progress. But in fact the governments that did make progress in these countries were also re-elected once.

Frameworks of Reform

The reform landscape contains features that are reasonably similar between OECD countries, such as the mechanisms of the political arena, public opinion and the media, special interests and civil servants. These features act and interact in certain ways, which have to be acknowledged by reformers and handled in the reform process. But a few features may differ more between countries and may affect the likelihood of reforms taking place. Some of these are capable of being influenced by politicians, in the long run at least. They can be referred to as general *frameworks of reform*—a number of institutions whose design will affect the incentives of reformers and the rules of the game:

1. A sound macroeconomic framework. Countries with a sound public budgetary balance have generally shown higher reform activity, while budgetary consolidation has tended to stall other reforms.[374]

---

[374] Höj et al (2006).

In recent decades, most OECD countries have gone from high inflation and large public budget deficits to low inflation and at least reasonably balanced budgets. The independence of central banks and the global financial markets have contributed to a more stable macroeconomic framework. And as politicians do not attempt to run the business cycle or have to manage short-term macroeconomic problems anymore, they can focus more on structural reforms.

2. New social pacts. A society with vast state interventions that seem to benefit several single special interests but are detrimental to society as a whole may be underpinned by an "iron triangle" of a few rent-seeking actors. But if one special interest changes its position, or if the government changes policy or a new force enters the game, the iron triangle may fall apart like a house of cards. Sometimes, business organisations have changed their position, which has been crucial.[375] At other times, the trade unions have. This has paved the way for new policies that previously seemed politically impossible, transforming the framework of social partners and facilitating reform.

3. International organisations. Membership of intergovernmental organisations like the EU, the OECD, the IMF and the World Bank will affect the framework. A country open to independent analysis, comparison, advice and competition is less likely to launch outright damaging policies. The international exchange of ideas, policies and advice leads to a normalisation of policies and institutions. The EU even issues and implements laws directly, which creates constraints, sometimes welcome, on national politics. Reform ideas and initiatives are sometimes "outsourced" to these organisations.

---

[375] Kerr (1998).

4. Constitutional setting. The very point of the constitutional framework is that politicians should not be able to change it easily. It provides limits for the state and rules for politics. But the lessons from different countries about how the various constitutional settings affect economic outcomes should not be ignored. Some constitutions encourage policies with a long-term aim of promoting the public good more than others. In constitutional transformations, governments might consider greater division of power, increased use of qualified majorities and measures to strengthen the independence of politicians from special interests.[376]

5. Independent ideas. Having a society with many independent researchers and opinion-formers, with a vibrant academic and public debate, is important to avoid policy mistakes and promote policy innovation. Independent universities and the existence of think-tanks and public committees may all play important roles in shaping new proposals, criticising the old order and paving the way for change. For a political movement, there will also be many measures in such a pluralistic society to change public opinion so as ultimately to change the course of politics.

6. Transparency and accountability. Many reforms have short-term costs and substantial long-term gains. But if reforms stall half-way or if they are only partially implemented (even initially) then the results may not materialise. This may happen if the politicians are "captured" along the way by special interests. Reforms that have no or limited positive effects will win little public support for the reformers. Governments may thus lose an election because of insufficient or slow reform. Measures to increase the transparency of public institutions and accountability of decision-makers can reduce the likelihood of politicians falling prey to special interests.[377]

---

[376] See, for example, Berggren (2003).

[377] Olofsgård (2003).

Methods of Reform

In a classic work entitled "Privatisation", Dr Madsen Pirie lists a number of main methods that can be and have been successfully used by reformers.[378] Depending on the specific reform and the general conditions, they are fairly general and can be applied in any OECD country. They cover major reforms such as the sale of state-owned companies, introduction of competition in public services, deregulation, dealing with special interests and the introduction of private funding in social security and welfare services. Almost 20 years old, these *reform methods* are to some extent related to the debates and reforms of that era, but they are largely timeless. Many problems remain to be solved and where there are new problems, old methods may still work. The list covers 21 separate methods, but they may be condensed somewhat and also supplemented by a few new examples:

1. Selling state-owned activities. Different reasons may exist for selling publicly owned activities, for example increasing competition, improving management or increasing citizens' ownership. Special interests will oppose it. A variety of implementation methods exist depending on the activity and situation. The entire business may be sold or only a proportion. A state-owned company can be sold to a large private buyer or to management or indeed the employees. Alternatively, it may be distributed to the citizens. After all, state-owned activities are often said to belong to the people.[379]

2. Private provision, public funding. Competition brings innovation, variety, improvements and lower costs. Increased competition is necessary in publicly provided services and this can be achieved

---

[378] Pirie (1988).

[379] A detailed and well-argued case for distributing state-owned companies in Sweden to citizens and giving people more control over their pensions can be found in Kling (2007).

by several methods. One way is to contract the provision of pub-licly funded services to private providers, for example by tenders (preferably on an international market). At least more peripheral parts of public services, such as maintenance, can be privately pro-vided directly. Another way is to introduce vouchers, which give choice to citizens and open up for competition.

3. Interest groups. Special interests cannot be allowed to stop reforms that would be in the general interest. But to facilitate reform—to defuse the opposition—the special interests can be "bought out" by some measure over a limited time. If subsidies are cut, for example, and people stand to lose their jobs they can be offered economic compensation. Thus, "going with the grain" simplifies reform. Compensation must, however, be quite limited or else provide special interests in other sectors with incentives to block reforms just to receive compensation.[380] Another way to handle special interests is to encourage new interest groups based on the future winners of reform. An association of private health care providers, for example, can balance the association of public health care providers.

4. Private funding. Dr Pirie wrote: *"For goods or services which are 'free', that is, financed out of general taxation, the demand is poten-tially infinite. It is in everyone's interest to consume individually as much as possible of goods which are paid for collectively."* This might be referred to as a "politics failure". Direct charging for some public services is one way to solve this. Other ways to bring in economic efficiency would be to abolish any restrictions for private funding, via foundations or financial markets, for example. Providing people with a right to buy a private solution instead of the offered public one and then billing the state is another way. Or indeed to allow "exit" in the form of tax deductions for people who purchase

---

[380] Castro & Coen-Pirani (2001).

private welfare or social insurance since they no longer consume the public services to the same extent.

5. Deregulation. Many regulations are directly harmful and have never come into existence in the first place for the benefit of the public good. There may be several ways to deregulate. One main path is for the state to actively simplify regulations or decrease their number. Another way would be to allow self-regulations by those affected in certain branches or areas. Another way is to use a "sunset" clause: if the continued existence of a regulation cannot be justified after a certain date it will be automatically removed. Closure proceedings could be used for state-owned companies in trouble just as for private companies.

6. Management. A tax-funded service will gain its funding independently of the decisions or actions by the consumers of that service. Contrary to the private sector, adapting to the demands of consumers in competition with others is a mechanism usually not present in the public sector. The incentives to adapt efficiently to consumers are weak. Apart from introducing competition, there are management changes within the public sector that could improve the incentives. The funding could be tied to measures of performance in relation to consumers.

7. Alternatives. Part of the resistance to change, despite sometimes apparent problems, is that we know what we have but cannot see what we will possibly get instead. However, there are ways to show what could be achieved instead, with reform. If formal public monopolies are abolished, new and emerging alternative institutions in, for example, education or health care can be encouraged. As they grow, they can provide positive examples. Small-scale experiments can also be tried, in a part of society, before reforms are launched on a wider scale. Also, harmful state interventions have often increased in times of crisis.

Reform Strategy

A reform can be described as being shaped and taking place in different steps. For a politician intent on pursuing reforms, there are *reform phases* of initiation, mobilisation, finalisation and implementation. This is a simplification that cannot be interpreted too literally, and sometimes things happen in slightly different ways. But it may be relevant as a mindset and no reform can take place without one of these phases. A reform strategy can also be referred to as either *activist*—pursuing a number of far-reaching reforms, perhaps breaking new ground—or *adaptive*—launching a number of reforms more reactively to adapt to what other countries have already done. The activist strategy is of course bolder, but both require reforms.[381] Of course, launching reforms is to some extent about political leadership: shaping proposals, working for a specific aim, setting the agenda, mobilising supporters and facing opponents. But strategic lessons may decide whether an effort to reform will be successful or not. Drawing a number of conclusions for a politician from the need for reform, countries that accomplished a lot, the political arena and evidence about how to do it, the strategic steps may be described as following these phases of reform:

1. Mandate for change. Politicians need a mandate for reform. Promising before an election to do nothing and suddenly doing a lot when in office (which has been referred to as "reform by stealth") is a fairly certain way to fail. The results will be justified objections, a limited likelihood of re-election and probable substantial opposition to any reforms. If the country is faced with a number of familiar problems, there may be scope to gain a general mandate for change. Should only a few problems be apparent, the problem issue has to be "isolated" and reform proposals

---

[381] Möller (2001).

focused on that area.[382] Everything that may be done in four or five years cannot be foreseen or communicated in advance. But if reforms are the aim, this has to be communicated.

2. Practical and pragmatic. A myriad of methods exists for gaining confidence and support when promising change. The reforms have to be realistic and not oversold by promising too much. Arguments for proposals can be ideological if the ideological standpoint is likely to be shared by most citizens. In other cases, the arguments should be more pragmatic.[383] Popular proposals presented by opponents or others who have influenced the agenda can be overtaken in a so-called triangulation strategy.

3. Decisive. A reformist politician has to have long-term aims and stick with them. He or she must have a strong will and be persistent. Changes of message, policy content or reform pace or direction will produce uncertainty, which is a threat to reform success. This does not mean that politicians should be deaf to public opinion (minor alterations may be relevant) but people will only support changes if it is apparent that the politician personally believes in them.

4. Size and package. One single reform will never be enough. There has to be a package of reforms with comprehensive solutions to problems or future challenges. The package should aim at changing incentives in the system so it operates more effectively. The reforms need to be substantial enough to produce visible results. A reform that is half-hearted or a compromise with special interests will fail—it has to go all the way. The reform process also has to be kept going and not lose steam.

5. Consistent. For a reform team to be able to launch and defend an agenda of change, it must have a united view of the mission and

---

[382] Schenström (2007).

[383] Eiken (2007).

values. There should be a deep sense, more than in words, about the direction and the means to use. This will ensure that actions and communication remain consistent, even as time passes. This is not only important for everyday work and the ability to launch new proposals in the same direction, but also for external credibility.[384]

6. No consensus. It might seem logical to build a broad political consensus for a reform proposal, thereby creating a stable future support. This has happened on a few occasions in various countries. But usually reforms are just delayed or watered down by a far-reaching consensus process. Most have been launched with more limited political support and have then become generally accepted after implementation. The lasting support for a more substantial change is thus achieved.

7. Sequencing. Evidence suggests there would be benefits in initiating reforms first in product markets and then in labour markets. According to the reformist finance minister of New Zealand, Roger Douglas, that sequencing is "fundamentally irrelevant" ideas by "armchair theorists".[385] It is very hard to plan, wait and launch reforms just as you wish. The situation is always changing. Unless there is action at the time given, the whole opportunity might be lost. Reforms that produce quick results are desirable but there is no reason to wait with other reforms.

8. Speed. Reforms should be quick enough to produce substantial positive effects before the next election. Thus, there are good reasons to launch them shortly after the previous election. A compromise is necessary with the chances of communicating with the public, which takes time. But reforms cannot wait for everyone to

---

[384] The importance of consistency between mission and values in any organisation that wishes to succeed well is described thoroughly in Welch, Jack, Winning, Haper Collins 2005.

[385] Douglas (1998).

understand every part. If there was a risk of reform withdrawal by going too fast, it might be better to slow down.[386] That risk, however, should be weighed against the likelihood of stalling the entire reform process, which is a greater threat. As Mart Laar, former Estonian prime minister, has pointed out: "As reforms are always unpopular, it is better to do them at once."[387]

9. Support. Political equilibrium theory suggests that an established order might change substantially if it is challenged. There are many ways of mobilising support for proposals and consistent communication is essential. Switzerland's interior minister, Pascal Couchepin, has remarked: *People have to listen to a hundred different voices. What is important is who they trust.*"[388] To reach a "tipping point" where a struggle for support may mobilise large groups, it is important to identify the small groups that are strongly engaged and that influence others.[389] Alliances in a broader movement are also relevant, though not allied to special interests benefiting from the current order.

10. Implementation. The procedure of implementation is very different between countries, with differing roles of public institutions and varying degrees of centralisation and administrative efficiency. A reform decision is, however, worthless if implementation fails. Securing implementation by the public institutions from the very start is therefore essential, especially since there will probably be resistance from at least some parts of the civil service.

11. Further reform. Although reforms are usually not reversed, they cannot be considered entirely safe just by being implemented. There is need to continue to defend what has been done. The most important reason for doing so might be that by defending

---

[386] Merlevede & Schoors (2005).

[387] Laar, Mart, E-mail interview, May 22nd 2007.

[388] Couchepin (2007).

[389] Gladwell (2000).

past reforms—and consistently pointing to their positive effects—there will be a case and credibility for further reforms in the future.

Every country needs reform, and every country can reform. The positive results in countries that have accomplished a lot are quite astonishing. A number of lessons can be drawn about what to do and, above all, how to do it. Re-election, recognition and real results are some incentives for politicians to actually reform. An agenda for reform should contain clear aims, a number of policy changes, appropriate methods and strategic components. It is to some extent about leadership, which is easier today than a few decades ago since the road to reform has been cleared. It is all about deciding to go in the reform direction.

EPILOGUE

A GENTLE BREEZE SWEPT OVER the field, rustling the colourful leaves on the trees. It was early autumn but the air was still warm and there were sounds of birds in the distance. A small wooden branch cracked as the former prime minister unintentionally stepped on it.

He was on a long walk in the countryside. Together with his wife—still married to him after more than three decades and a hectic political life—he had bought a modest cottage and spent a good deal of time there in the last few months. The grandchildren were frequent visitors.

He enjoyed his new life. It seemed amazing that he was able to decide all by him self what he wanted to do tomorrow—or next week. He had politely turned down offers about new professional positions, except occasional writing and speaking engagements on how to achieve real change in society.

More than two years had passed since he resigned as prime minister and party leader. Four years had passed since the party congress, the one occasion he always pointed to as the main decisive moment when the country's development was turned around.

Quite a number of retired prime ministers in other countries were good friends. They shared experiences and understood each other, despite different party affiliations. All felt relieved not to be prime minister any more, but some were more proud of their past than others. A few were slightly bitter.

This former prime minister was quite comfortable. A number of actions in his career had been regrettable, particularly in his first years of office. The heat of the political battle had sometimes led him to be short-sighted. Some statements and policies had been damaging. But when he resigned, some remarkable achievements could be attributed to his efforts.

At the podium four years ago, he could have heard a needle drop anywhere in the vast conference hall. After the usual greetings, some jokes at opponents' expense and an international overview, he had delivered a message of change. The initially cheerful and slightly nervous delegates had turned completely silent, as if waiting.

The tension could have been cut with a knife. The prime minister surprised some by not proposing that many or as drastic changes as the initial speculation had suggested. But he argued for further product market deregulation, quite bold tax reforms and, above all, a series of labour market reforms. He also outlined some long-term constitutional changes.

In the speech, he had not only delivered emotional arguments and compelling facts. He made reform seem like a logical step consistent with the roots of his party as well as with the foundations of the country. Change was an opportunity and reform was an historic quest. The country could reach higher and farther. He had put his soul into every sentence.

It had started somewhere in the back, to the left from his viewpoint. A silence of at least 20 minutes was broken by a spontaneous applause. Slowly, as if it was necessary to be cautious, the applause spread through the hall. Some delegates did not join in, but many were enthusiastic. It was almost as if a spell had been lifted.

No delegate had been really surprised by the new policies. The proposals had been part of public debate for years and the subject of internal party studies. It seemed as if the only doubt was whether someone would dare to take on the leadership role. When that happened, all that was left for the delegates was to relate to the new position.

And they did. Many had been longing for a proactive policy, setting the agenda and solving problems in society rather than denying them. They became convinced that reforms were in the interest not only of the country but of the party, and therefore themselves. Support for the traditional wing of the party that opposed reforms, after all, turned out to be quite limited.

The reform proposals were well-founded and thoroughly prepared. By international comparison they were not particularly radical. Other countries had done similar things. So success seemed guaranteed. Most experts had lined up to support the reforms, some arguing that more should be done, others voicing marginal criticism.

During his walk, the former prime minister had climbed a hill from which he had a nice view of the landscape. He gazed into the distance. This view had probably not changed much for a century, he thought, but it seemed different from just four years ago. It was probably just his own feeling, but the landscape seemed to be more open and welcoming.

There had been criticism and protests against the reforms. The trade unions, traditionally close to his party, had staged demonstrations. But the government stayed on course, arguing for the general good. The protests turned out to be quite short-lived. Most people later seemed pleased that the trade unions had become more loosely tied to the party.

Just one year after the reforms were introduced he had resigned, as planned. The woman who was now the party leader and prime minister was previously finance minister. Responsible for several of the reforms, she had been challenged in the leadership election but secured victory by a comfortable margin.

The government had been re-elected two years later, though this time had formed a coalition with a centrist party. It was committed to finalising the previous reforms and to initiating further reform to improve welfare services and social security.

The former prime minister walked across an old stone bridge. He kept returning to thoughts about human nature, society and politics. Paradoxically, everything seemed both immensely complex and quite simple. Politics was truly an art of the possible—and more seemed possible than was sometimes understood.

As the first reforms were launched, the criticism from many directions increased. Regrettably, the government had compromised on some tax reforms and lost reformist momentum. But several product markets had been deregulated and the labour market reforms were pursued with all possible strength.

Four years later, there had been results. No revolution, but a notable increase in employment levels. There was a debate about the causes and, sure, the economic upswing had played a role. But the improvement was there nonetheless. This was especially true for young people and immigrants. The reforms had attracted praise from several international organisations.

The opposition Christian Democrats had never recovered from being perceived as reactive and defensive after the government's bold reform move. They had lost some of their policy proposals and though they gained slightly in the election were still in opposition. It seemed likely, though, that sooner or later they would make a bold move too.

Public opinion had changed on a number of counts. Value surveys showed that people still valued social safety, but its definition had changed. Work was considered more important than before. Optimism about the future had picked up. The former prime minister thought that he had contributed to a new definition of a "social model"—one that embraced change.

His popularity had actually peaked before the reforms. On his resignation, polls showed that people respected him, but not much more. This did not discomfort him. He knew that no politician finished as a hero and that his efforts would in time be judged by history against the background of his legacy of change and its increasingly positive effects.

Two of the closest neighbouring countries had been inspired by the reforms, recently launching similar proposals. The former prime minister could not help but reflect that he and his colleagues had redefined the agenda not only of his party, but also of the country and of several other countries too.

As he entered his warm cottage, his eyes fell on the running shoes lying at the door. He had not been jogging for a long time due to a knee injury. But he always kept the shoes there, as a rather silly joke to himself. They had a famous trademark with an inspiring catch-phrase:

"Just do it!"

REFERENCES

Abrams, Burton (1999), "The Effect of Government Size on the Unemployment Rate." *Public Choice,* vol 99, June.

Afonso, António, Schuknecht, Ludger & Tanzi, Vito (2003), Public Sector Efficiency : An International Comparison. Frankfurt am Main: European Central Bank, (ECB Working Paper 242).

Ågerup, Martin (2007), "Myten om Flexicurity." Lecture at a seminar arranged by Timbro, April 17th.

Ahlin, Åsa (2003), "Does School Competition Matter? : Effects of Large-Scale School Choice Reform on Student Performance." Uppsala: Department of Economics, Uppsala University (Working paper).

Ahmed, Shagil (1986), "Temporary and Permanent Government Spending in an Open Economy." *Journal of Monetary Economics,* March.

Alesina, Alberto et al (1999), Fiscal Policy, Profits and Investment. Cambridge, MA: National Bureau of Economic Research, NBER (Working Paper 7207).

Alesina, Alberto & Spolaore, Enrico (2003), *The Size of Nations.* Cambridge, MA: MIT Press.

Alesina, Alberto & Glaeser, Edward (2004), *Fighting Poverty in the US and in Europe : A World of Difference.* Oxford: Oxford University Press.

Alesina, Alberto & Giavazzi, Francesco (2006), *The Future of Europe : Reform or Decline.* Cambridge, MA: The MIT Press.

Andersson-Skog, Lena & Krantz, Olle, eds (2002), *Omvandlingens sekel.* Lund: Studentlitteratur, pp 11–39.

Åslund, Anders (2007a), *Building Capitalism : The Transformation of the Former Soviet Bloc.* New rev ed. Cambridge/New York: Cambridge University Press.

Åslund, Anders (2007b), "How Can the EU Emulate the Positive Features of the East Asian Model?" Washington, DC: Peterson Institute for International Economics, March 23rd, <www.case.com.pl/plik--14184054.pdf?nlang=710>.

Baily, Martin L & Farrell, Diana (2005), "A Road Map for European Economic Reform." *The McKinsey Quarterly,* September.

Baily, Martin & Farrell, Diana (2006), "Breaking Down Barriers to Growth." *Finance & Development* (IMF), March.

Baldwin, Richard (2006), "Globalisation : the Great Unbundling(s)." Helsinki: Economic Council of Finland (Globalisation Changes for Europe and Finland), September.

Barber, Tony & Michaels, Adrian (2007), "In For a Trim : An Italy Anxious For Growth Tries To Stimulate Competition." *Financial Times,* 28th February, <www.ft.com/cms/s/b2e1dbca-c6d0-11db-8f4f-000b5df10621.html>.

Bardach, Eugene (2005), *A Practical Guide for Policy Analysis.* New York/London: Chatham House Publishers.

Bartholomée, Yvette & Maarse, Hans (2006), "Health Insurance reform in the Netherlands." *Eurohealth*, vol 12, no 2, pp 7–9.

Barysch, Katinka (2006), "Enlargement Two Years On : Economic Success or Political Failure?" London: Centre for European Reform, April (Briefing paper for the Confederation of Danish Industries and the Central Organization of Industrial Employees in Denmark).

Bas, Jacobs & van der Ploeg, Frederick (2005), "Guide to Reform of Higher Education : A European Perspective." London: Centre for Economic Policy Research, November (Discussion Paper 5327).

Bassanini, Andrea & Scarpetta, Stefano (2001), "The Driving Forces of Economic Growth : Panel Data Evidence for the OECD Countries." Paris: OECD (OECD Economic Studies no 33).

Bassanini, Andrea & Duval, Romain (2006), *Employment Patterns in OECD Countries : Reassessing the Role of Policies and Institutions.* Paris: Organisation of Economic Cooperation and Development, June (OECD Economics Department Working Paper no 486).

Baumol, William J (1967), "Macroeconomics of Unbalanced Growth : The Anatomy of Urban Crises." *The American Economic Review,* vol 57, no 3.

Baumol, William J, Blackman, S A B & Wolff, E N (1985), "Unbalanced Growth revisited : Asympotic Stagnancy and New Evidence." *The American Economic Review,* vol 75, no 4.

Baumol, William J (2002), *The Free-Market Innovation Machine.* Princeton, NJ: Princeton University Press.

Bayoumi, Tamim, Laxton, Douglas & Pesenti, Paolo (2004), "Benefits and Spillovers of Greater Competition in Europe : A Macroeconomic Assessment." New York: Federal Reserve Bank of New York, April (Staff Report 182).

Berggren, Niclas (2003), "The Frailty of Economic Reforms : Political Logic and Constitutional Lessons." Stockholm: The Ratio Institute (Ratio Working Papers 1).

Bergh, Andreas (2006), "Explaining Welfare State Survival : The Role of Economic Freedom and Globalization," Stockholm: The Ratio Institute (Ratio Working Papers 101).

Bessard, Pierre (2007), "The Swiss Tax System : Key Features and Lessons for Policy Makers." Alexandria, VA: Center for Freedom and Prosperity, February (*Prosperitas*).

Bianchi, Marco, Gudmundsson, Bjorn R & Zoega, Gylfi (2000), "Iceland's Natural Experiment In Supply-Side Economics." London: Centre for Economic Policy Research, January (Discussion Paper 2367).

Birkland, Thomas A (2005), *An Introduction to the Policy Process : Theories, Concepts, and Models of Public Policy Making.* 2nd ed. Armonk, NY: M E Sharpe, 2005.

Björnskov, Christian & Foss, Nicolai J (2006), "Economic Freedom and Entrepreneurial Activity : Some Cross-Country Evidence." Aalborg: Copenhagen business School, DRUID (Econ Papers 06–18).

Blair, Tony (2007), "What I've Learned." *The Economist,* 4th June.

Blank, Rebecca M & Schoeni, Robert F (2003), "Changes in the Distribution of Children's Family Income over the 1990's." Washington, DC: American Economic Association, January 2003 (Paper for the Annual Meeting).

Blank, Rebecca M (2004), "Evaluating Welfare Reform in the United States." Cambridge, MA: National Bureau of Economic Research, June (NBER Working Paper 8983).

Blundell, John (2005), *Waging the War of Ideas.* London: The Institute of Economic Affairs.

Boeri, Tito (2004), What Are the Options for Pension and Social reforms in Europe? Steyning, UK: Wilton Park Conferences, May (Paper presented at the 747th Conference).

Bosma, Niels & Harding, Rebecca (2006), "GEM 2006 Results." *Global Entrepreneurship Monitor.*

Botero, Juan C et al (2004), "The Regulation of Labor." *The Quatrely Journal of Economics,* November.

Bradford, Scott C, Grieco, Paul L E & Hufbauer, Gary Clyde (2006), "The Payoff to America From Globalization." *The World Economy,* vol 29, no 7.

Brooks, David (2006), "The Populist Myths on Income Inequality." *New York Times,* September 7th.

Buchanan, James M (2000–), *The Collected Works of James M Buchanan.* Indianapolis, IN: The Liberty Fund (The Library of Economics and Liberty), <www.econlib.org/library/Buchanan/buchCContents.html>.

Böhlmark, Anders & Lindahl, Mikael (2007), "The Impact of School Choice on Pupil Achievement, Segregation and Costs : Swedish Evidence." Bonn: The Institute for the Study of Labour, May (IZA Discussion Paper 2786).

Cameron, David (2006), "David Cameron's speech at Google Zeitgeist Europe 2006." *Guardian Unlimited,* 22nd May.

Caplan, Bryan (2007), "The Myth of the Rational Voter : Why Democracies Choose Bad Policies." Washington, DC: Cato Institute (Policy Analysis May 29th).

Capretta, James C (2007), "Global Aging and the Sustainability of Public Pensions Systems." Washington, DC: Center for Strategic and International Studies, CSIS, January.

Carlin, Wendy et al (2001), "Competition and Enterprise Performance in Transition Economies : Evidence From a Cross-Country Survey." London: Centre for Economic Policy Research, June (CEPR Discussion Paper 2840).

Carlstrom, Charles T & Gokhale, Jagadeesh (1991), "Government Consumption, Taxation, and Economic Activity." *Economic Review,* 3rd Quarter, vol 27, no 3. Cleveland, OH: Federal Reserve Bank of Cleveland.

Castro, Rui L de & Coen-Pirani, Daniele (2001), "On the Political Economy of Sequential Reforms." Montreal: Université de Montreal, Département de Sciences Economiques (Cachiers de Recheche, 2001-21).

Central Statistical Organisation, India, Website. New Delhi: Ministry of Statistics and Programme Implementation, <http://mospi.nic.in/cso_test1.htm>.

Cheibub, José Antonio (2006), *Presidentialism, Parliamentarism and Democracy.* Cambridge/New York: Cambridge University Press.

CIA (2007), *World Factbook 2007.* Washington, DC: The Central Intelligence Agency, <www.cia.gov/library/publications/the-world-factbook/>.

Civitas (2002), "The Swiss Health Care System." London: The Institute for the Study of Civil Society, <www.civitas.org.uk/pdf/Switzerland.pdf>.

Clausewitz, Carl von (1984), *On War.* Edited and translated by Michael Howard and Peter Paret. Princeton, NJ: Princeton University Press.

Clinton, Bill (2004), *My Life.* New York: Knopf.

Collier, Paul & Dollar, David (2002), *Globalization, Growth, and Poverty : Building an Inclusive World Economy.* Washington, DC: World Bank/New York: Oxford University Press.

Conway, P, Janod, V & Nicoletti, G (2005), *Product Market Regulation in OECD Countries : 1998 to 2003.* Paris: Organisation for Economic Cooperation and Development (OECD Economics Department Working Paper 419).

Cotis, Jean-Philippe (2007), Speech at a Conference on Economic Reform arranged by The Confederation of Swedish Enterprise, Stockholm, July 9th.

Couchepin, Pascal (2007), Interviewed by Johnny Munkhammar, May 4th.

Crawford, Leslie (2005), "Amnesty Fails to Ease Spanish Worries Over Immigration." *Financial Times,* May 9th, <www.ft.com/cms/s/0/107c62c2-c026-11d9-b376-00000e2511c8.html>.

Crosby, Lyndon (2006), "John Howard Implements Unpopular Policies and Makes Them Popular." *The Telegraph,* August 6th.

Dahl, Robert (1989), *Democracy and Its Critics.* New Haven: Yale University.

Daily Telegraph (2001), "Persson Non Grata." June 16th.

Daveri, Francesco & Tabellini, Guido (1997), "Unemployment, Growth and Taxation in Industrial Countries." London: Centre for Economic Policy Research, August (Discussion Paper 1681).

David, Paul A (2000), "Path Dependence, Its Critics and the Quest for 'Historical Economics'," in P Garrouste & S Ioannides, eds, *Evolution and Path Dependence In Economic Ideas : Past and Present.* Cheltenham, UK: Edward Elgar.

Davis, Steven J & Henrekson, Magnus (2005), "Tax Effects on Work Activity, Industry Mix and Shadow Economy Size : Evidence From Rich-Country Comparisons," in R Goméz-Salvador et al (eds), *Labour Supply and Incentives to Work in Europe.* Aldershot: Edward Elgar.

De Santis, Roberta, Mercuri, Christina M & Vicarelli, Claudio (2001), "Taxes and Location of Foreign Direct Investments : An Emprirical Analysis for the European Union Countries." Rome: Instituto di Studi e Analisi Economica, ISAE, November (ISAE Working Papers 24).

De Soto, Hernando (2000), *The Mystery of Capital.* New York: Basic Books.

Dilip, Das K (2006), "Globalization in the World of Finance." *Global Economy Journal,* vol 6, Issue 1.

Dillard, Dudley (1967), *Economic Development of the North-Atlantic Community.* Englewood Cliffs, NJ: Prentice Hall.

Docteur, Elisabeth & Oxley, Howard (2003), *Health-Care Systems : Lessons From the Reform Experience.* Paris: Organisation for Economic Cooperation and Development (Economics department Working Paper 374), December 3rd, <www.oecd.org/dataoecd/5/53/22364122.pdf>.

Doing Business Project, "Employing Workers." Washington, DC: The World Bank/The International Finance Corporation, <www.doingbusiness.org/ExploreTopics/EmployingWorkers/>.

Doing Business Report (2005), *Removing Obstacles to Growth.* Washington, DC: The World Bank/The International Finance Corporation/Oxford University Press, <www.doingbusiness.org/documents/DoingBusiness2005.PDF>.

Douglas, Roger (1998), "Evaluation Criteria of Successful Economic Reform." Prague: Liberální Institut, October (Annual Lecture).

Drazen, David W (2004), "The Outsourcing Bogeyman." *Foreign Affairs,* May/June.

EBRD (2007), *People in Transition.* London: European Bank for Reconstruction and Development, May (Transition Report 2007).

The Economist (2002), "Model Makers : Survey of The Netherlands." May 2nd.

The Economist (2004a), "A Special Case : Survey of Switzerland." February 12th.

The Economist (2004b), "The Second Transition." June 24th.

The Economist (2004c), "The Luck of the Irish : Survey." October 14th.

The Economist (2005a), "Jacques Chirac and the Tobin Tax." January 27th.

The Economist (2005b), "Has He Got the Ticker?" May 5th.

The Economist (2005c), "Addio, Dolce Vita : Survey of Italy." November 24th.

The Economist (2006a), "Waiting for a Wunder : Survey of Germany." February 9th.

The Economist (2006b), "The Art of the Impossible : Survey of France." October 26th.

The Economist (2006c), "Shadows at Europe's Heart." October 26th.

The Economist (2007a), "Britannia Redux : Survey of Britain." February 1st.

The Economist (2007b), "Browned Off." February 1st.

The Economist (2007c), "The Quest for Prosperity." March 15th.

The Economist (2007d), "Lexington." June 2nd–8th.

The Economist (2007e), "Charlemagne : The Summit Dances." June 23rd.

The Economist (2007f), "British Manufacturing : In Praise of Shopkeepers and Sellers." June 23rd.

The Economist (2007g), "Worrying About a Crash." July 7th.

The Economist (2007h), "Where Money Seems to Talk." July 7th.

The Economist (2007i), "Denmark : Country Briefing." September 8th, <www.economist.com/countries/Denmark/>.

Edwards, John (2006), *Quiet Boom : How the Long Economic Upswing Is Changing Australia and the World.* Double Bay, New South Wales: Lowy Institute for International Policy (Lowy Institute Paper 14), 2006.

Ehrenkrona, Olof (2006), Power point presentation at Post Election Conference, September 28th–29th, 2006, at Lejondal. Stockholm: Timbro.

Ehrlich, Isaac & Jinyoung, Kim (2005), "Social Security, Demographic Trends, and Economic Growth : Theory and Evidence From the International Experience." Boston, MA: National Bureau of Economic Research, February (Working Paper 11121).

Eigen, Lewis D & Siegel, Jonathan P (2003), *The Macmillan Dictionary of Political Quotations.* London: Macmillan.

Eiken, Odd (2007), Interviewed by Johnny Munkhammar, March 30th.

Engen, Eric M & Skinner, Jonathan (1992), "Fiscal Policy and Economic Growth." Cambridge, MA: National Bureau of Economic Research (NBER Working Paper 4223).

Erixon, Fredrik (forthcoming), *The Baltic Tiger : The Political Economy of Estonia's Transition From Plan To Market.* Mimeo.

Esser, Frank & Pfetsch, Barbara, eds (2004), *Comparing Political Communication*, New York: Cambridge University Press.

Estonian Information Centre (2007), *Environmental Review 2005 : Indicator-Based Summary.* Tallinn, <www.keskkonnainfo.ee/uudised/226/ylevaade.pdf>.

EU KLEMS Database (2007), "Productivity in the European Union : A Comparative Industry Approach." Groeningen: University of Groeningen (EU KLEMS2003), <www.euklems.net/index.html>.

Euromonitor International (2006), *World Income Distribution 2006/2007.* London.

European Central Bank (2007), "The Enlarged EU and Euro Area Economies." *ECB Monthly Bulletin,* January 2007, <www.ecb.int/pub/pdf/mobu/mb200701en.pdf>.

European Commission (2006a), "Eurobarometer 66 : Public Opinion in the European Union." Brussels: December, <www.europa-kommissionen.dk/upload/application/2f76b69d/uuu.pdf>.

European Commission (2006b), "Statistical Annex of European Economy : Autumn 2006." Brussels/Luxembourg: Economic and Financial Affairs, Directorate General (DG ECFIN), <http://ec.europa.eu/economy_finance/publications/european_economy/statisticalannex0206_en.htm>.

European Commission (2006c), "The Macroeconomic effects of the Single Market Programme After 10 Years." Brussels, May 16th, <http://ec.europa.eu/internal_market/10years/background_en.htm>.

European Commission (2006d), *Enlargement, Two Years After : An Economic Evaluation.* Brussels: Bureau of European Policy Advisers, and Directorate-General for Economic and Financial Affairs, May (European Economy, Occasional Papers, No 24), <http://ec.europa.eu/economy_finance/publications/occasional_papers/2006/ocp24en.pdf>.

European Commission (2007a), "A Single Market for the Citizens : Interim Report to the 2007 Spring European Council." Brussels: Energy and Transport/Directorate General (Brussels, 21.2.2007, COM(2007) 60 final), <http://eur-lex.europa.eu/LexUriServ/site/en/com/2007/com2007_0060en01.pdf>.

European Commission (2007b), Collection of documents on European gas and electricity. Brussels: Directorate General for Energy and Transport, <http://ec.europa.eu/energy/gas/publications/index_en.htm>.

European Environment Agency (2005), *The European Environment : State and Outlook 2005.* Copenhagen, <http://reports.eea.europa.eu/state_of_environment_report_2005_1/en>.

Eurostat (1996), "Real GDP Growth Rate." Luxemburg, <http://epp.eurostat.ec.europa.eu/portal/page?_pageid=1996,39140985&_dad=portal&_schema=PORTAL&screen=detailref&language=en&product=STRIND_ECOBAC&root=STRIND_ECOBAC/ecobac/eb012>.

Eurostat (2007), "Euro area unemployment stable at 6.9%." Luxemburg, (Euro Indicators News Release 118/2007), <http://epp.eurostat.ec.europa.eu/pls/portal/docs/PAGE/PGP_PRD_CAT_PREREL/PGE_CAT_PREREL_YEAR_2007/PGE_CAT_PREREL_YEAR_2007_MONTH_08/3-31082007-EN-BP.PDF>.

Farazmand, Ali (2003), "Chaos and Transformation Theories : A Theoretical Analysis with Implications for Organization Theory and Public Management." *Public Organization Review, A Global Journal,* no 3.

Feld, Lars P, Zimmerman, Horst & Döring, Thomas (2004), "Federalism, Decentralization and Economic Growth." Marburg, Germany: Philipps-Universität.

Feldt, Kjell-Olof (1991), *Alla dessa dagar : i regeringen 1982–1990.* Stockholm: Norstedts.

Fernández, Cristina & Ortega, A Carolina (2006), "Labour Market Assimilation of Immigrants in Spain : Employment at the Expense of Bad Job Matches?" Barcelona: IESE Business School, University of Navarra, September (Working Paper D/644).

Florida, Richard (2002), *The Rise of the Creative Class.* New York: Basic Books.

Fogel, Robert W (1999), "Catching Up With the Economy." *The American Economic Review,* vol 89, no 1, March.

Francois, Joseph, F & Schuknecht, Ludger (1999), "Trade In Financial Services : Procompetitive Effects And Growth Performance." London: Centre for Economic Policy Research, December (Discussion Paper 2144).

Freedom House (2007), *Freedom in the World 2007.* New York, <www.freedomhouse.org>.

Friedman, Thomas (2005), *The World is Flat*. New York: Farrar, Straus and Giroux.

Frijters, Paul & Gregory, Bob (2006), "From Golden Age to Golden Age : Australia's 'Great Leap Forward'." Bonn: Institute for the Study of Labor (IZA DP 2068).

Fu, Dong, Taylor, Lori L & Yücel, Mine K (2003), "Fiscal Policy and Growth." Dallas, TX: Federal Reserve Bank of Dallas (Working Paper 0301).

Fundación FAES (2006), "The Indicators of Change : Spain 1996–2004." Madrid: Fundación Para el Analysisy los Estudios Sociales, <www.fundacionfaes.org>.

Gaynor, Martin, Haas-Wilson, Debroah & Vogt, William B (1998), "Are Invisible Hands Good Hands? : Moral Hazard, Competition, and the Second-Best in Health Care Markets." Cambridge, MA: National Bureau of Economic Research, December (NBER Working Paper 6865).

Gennser, Margit (2007), Interviewed by Johnny Munkhammar, July 2nd.

Gilpin, Robert (2001), *Global Political Economy : Understanding the International Economic Order*. Princeton, NJ: Princeton University Press.

Gissurarsson, Hannes H (2007), "The Icelandic Economic Miracle." Speech at a conference, "The Source of Wealth in Small States," organized by The University of Iceland, The Institute of International Affairs, September 14th.

Gladwell, Malcolm (2000), *The Tipping Point : How Little Things Can Make a Great Difference.* Boston: Little, Brown and Company.

Goklany, Indur (2006), *The Improving State of the World.* Washington, DC: Cato Institute.

Government of Australia, Website, "Choose Australia." Belcannon, ACT, <www.immi.gov.au/living-in-australia/choose-australia/index.htm>.

Government of The Netherlands (2007), "The New Care System in the Netherlands : Durability, Solidarity, Quality, Efficiency." The Hague: Ministry of Health, Welfare and Sport, <http://healthlaw.nl/healthcare_reform.pdf>.

Government of Sweden (1999), "Hur gör man? : Om sysselsättnings- och välfärdsreformer i fyra EU-länder." Åse Lidbeck, ed. Stockholm (Ds 1999:37), <www.regeringen.se/content/1/c4/37/44/66a20510.pdf>.

Guiso, Luigi, Sapienza, Paolo & Zingales, Luigi (2002), "People's Opium? : Religion and Economic Attitudes." London: Centre for Economic Policy Research, October (DEPR Discussion Paper 3588).

Hallin, Daniel C & Mancini, Paolo (2004), *Comparing Media Systems : Three Models of Media and Politics.* New York: Cambridge University Press.

Hansson, Åsa (2006), "Hur påverkar en skatt på arbetsutbudet och efterfrågan på arbetskraft?" Stockholm: Svenskt Näringsliv, September.

Hauptmeier, Sebastian, Heipertz, Martin & Schuknecht, Ludger (2006), "Expenditure Reform in Industrialised Countries : a Case Study Approach." Frankfurt am Main: European Central Bank, May (ECB Working Paper 634).

Hawksworth, John (2006), "The World in 2050 : How Big Will the Major Emerging Market Economies Get and How Can the OECD Compete?" New York: PricewaterhouseCoopers, March, <www.pwc.com/extweb/pwcpublications.nsf/docid/56DD37D0C3 99661D852571410060FF8B/$file/world2050emergingeconomies.pdf>.

Hayek, F A (1944), *The Road to Serfdom.* London: Routledge.

He, Jie (2007), "Environmental Impacts of Foreign Trade : The Case of Industrial Emission of Sulfur Dioxide (SO2) in Chinese Provinces." Sherbrooke, Canada: Université de Sherbrooke (Working Paper 07–02), <www.munkhammar.org/pdf/EnvImpChina.pdf>.

Health Consumer Powerhouse (2007), "Euro Health Consumer Index 2007." Brussels, <www.healthpowerhouse.com/media/Rapport_EHCI_2007.pdf>.

Hellman, Jonas & Rankka, Maria (1999), *Irland : Den globala ön.* Stockholm: Timbro.

Henderson, David (1996), "New Zealand in International Perspective." Wellington, NZ: New Zealand Business Roundtable, August, <www.nzbr.org.nz/documents/publications/dba-publications/ nz_international_perspective_1996.pdf>.

Higgs, Robert (1987), *Crisis and Leviathan : Critical Episodes in the Growth of American Government.* Oxford/New York: Oxford University Press/Pacific Institute for Public Policy.

Honohan, P, ed (1997), "EU Structural Funds in Ireland : A Mid-Term Evaluation of the CSF 1994–99." Dublin: The Economic and Social Research Institute, ESRI, <www.esri.ie/publications/search_for_a_publication/search_results/view/index.xml?id=485>.

HSBC (2007), "The Future of Retirement Study." London: HSBC Global Forum on Ageing and Retirement, <https://www.ageingforum.org/content/FutureOfRetirementProgrammeIntroductionText.aspx>.

Höj, Jens et al (2006), "The Political Economy of Structural Reform : Empirical Evidence From OECD Countries." Paris: Organisation for Economic Cooperation and Development, July 19th (OECD Economics Department Working Papers 501).

IMF (2007a), "World Economic and Financial Surveys," in *World Economic Outlook Database,* October, <www.imf.org/external/pubs/ft/weo/2007/02/weodata/index.aspx>.

IMF (2007b), *Spillovers and Cycles in the Global Economy.* Washington, DC: International Monetary Fund (World Economic Outlook, April 2007).

Immervoll, Herwig, et al (2004), "Welfare reform in European Countries : A Micro-Simulation Analysis." London: Centre for Economic Policy Research, March (Discussion Paper 4324).

Industry Commission (1998), "Commonwealth of Australia," in *Microeconomic Reforms in Australia: A Compendium From the 1970s to 1997.* Canberra, January (Research Paper AGPS).

IPRI (2007), *International Property Rights Index : 2007 Report.* Washington, DC, <http://internationalpropertyrightsindex.org/>.

Jackson, Richard & Howe, Neil (2003), *The 2003 Aging Vulnerability Index.* Washington, DC: Center for Strategic and International Studies, CSIS, <www.csis.org/media/csis/pubs/aging_index.pdf>.

Johansson, Dan (2004), "Skatternas utveckling, omfattning och fördelning," in Nils Karlson, ed, *Skatter och värdighet.* Stockholm: The Ratio Institute.

Johnson, Anders (2001), *Katekes för reformvänner.* Stockholm: Reforminstitutet.

Kane, Tim, Holmes, Kim R & O'Grady, Mary Anastasia (2007), *2007 Index of Economic Freedom.* Washington, DC: Heritage Foundation/Wall Street Journal.

Kangas, Olli, Lundberg, Urban & Ploug, Niels (2006), *Three Routes to a Pension Reform.* Stockholm: Institute for Futures Studies (Arbetsrapport 2006:10), <http://econpapers.repec.org/paper/hhsifswps/2006_5F010.htm>.

Kaplan, Richard (2005), "Who's Afraid of Personal Responsibility? : Health Savings Accounts and the Future of American Health Care." Champaign, IL: University of Illinois, College of Law (Law and Economics Working Paper LE05–025).

Karlson, Nils (2004), "Dignity and the Burden of the Welfare State." Stockholm: The Ratio Institute (Ratio Working Papers 34).

Karras, Georgios (1996), "The Optimal Government Size : Further International Evidence on the Productivity of Government Services." *Economic Inquiry,* vol 34, April.

Katz, Jesper (2006), "Häftig skatt eller sexig tillväxt." Stockholm: Timbro (Rapport).

Kearney, A T (2006), "Foreign Policy Globalization Index 2006." Chicago: Carnegie Endowment for International Peace, <www.atkearney.com/main.taf?p=5,4,1,116>.

Kerr, Roger (1998), "The Role of Business in Public Affairs : Some New Zealand Perspectives." Melbourne, Australia: New Zealand Business Roundtable, <www.nzbr.org.nz/documents/speeches/speeches-98/ role_of_business_in_public_affairs.pdf>.

Kerr, Roger (2005), "Lessons From Labour Market Reform in New Zealand." Lecture at The HR Nicholls Society's XXVI Conference in Melbourne, Australia, March 18th. Wellington: New Zealand Business Roundtable.

Keynes, John Maynard (1936), *General Theory of Employment, Interest and Money.* London: Macmillan.

Kim, Christine & Rector, Robert (2006), "Welfare Reform Turns Ten : Evidence Shows Reduced Dependence, Poverty." *Issues,* August 1st. Washington, DC: The Heritage Foundation, August 1st.

Kingdon, John W (2003), *Agendas, Alternatives, and Public Policies.* New York: Longman (Longman Classics in Political Science).

Kling, Dick (2007), *Radhusproletärer och ombudskapitalister.* Timbro Stockholm: Timbro.

Krueger, Anne O (1974), "The Political Economy of the Rent-Seeking Society." *The American Economic Review,* vol 64, no 3, June.

Kugler, Adriana, Jimeno-Serrano, Juan Francisco & Hernanz, Virginia (2003), "Employment Consequences of Restrictive Permanent Contracts : Evidence from Spanish Labour Market Reforms." London: Centre for Economic Policy Research, (Working Paper 3724).

Kurzweil, Ray (2005), *The Singularity Is Near : When Humans Transcend Biology.* London: Duckworth.

Kurzweil, Ray (2007), Website, <www.kurzweilai.net/>.

Laar, Mart (2007), E-mail interview by Johnny Munkhammar, May 22nd.

Landes, David S (1998), *The Wealth and Poverty of Nations.* New York: Norton.

Lang, Dany (2006), "Can the Danish Model of 'Flexicurity' Be a Matrix For the Reform of European Labour Markets?" Bordeaux and Toulouse: Groupement de Recherches Économiques et Sociales, GRES (Working Papers of GRES 2006-18), <www.gres-so.org>.

Lauback, Thomas & Wise, Michael (2005), "Product Market Competition and Economic Performance in Iceland." Paris: Organisation for Economic Cooperation and Development (OECD Economics Department Working Paper 426).

Layard, Richard (2005), *Happiness : Lessons From a New Science.* London: Allen Lane.

Legrain, Philippe (2007), *Immigrants : Your Country Needs Them.* Princeton, NJ: Princeton University Press.

Lindbeck, Assar & Snower, Dennis J (2002), "The Insider-Outsider Theory : A Survey." Bonn: The Institute for the Study of Labour, May (IZA Discussion Paper 534).

Lomborg, Björn (2001), *The Skeptical Environmentalist.* Cambridge/New York: Cambridge University Press.

Luttmer, Erzo F P (1998), "Group Loyalty and the Taste For Redistribution." Chicago: University of Chicago/The Harris School of Public Policy, <http://harrisschool.uchicago.edu/About/publications/ working-papers/pdf/wp_99_02.pdf>.

Luxembourg Income Study (2006), "Luxembourg Wealth Study : Final Beta Phase Conference." Luxembourg, July, <www.lisproject.org/lws.htm>.

Machiavelli, Niccolò (2005), *The Prince.* Oxford: Oxford University Press (first edition 1505).

McCombs, Maxwell (2004), *Setting the Agenda – The Mass Media and Public Opinion.* Oxford: Polity Press.

McCormick, John (2005), *Understanding the European Union : A Concise Introduction.* 3 ed. New York: Palgrave Macmillan,

McKinsey Global Institute (2003), "Improving European Competitiveness." *MGI Perspective,* July, <www.mckinsey.com/mgi/publications/european_competitiveness.asp>.

McKinsey Global Institute (2006), "Sweden's Economic Performance : Recent Developments, Current Priorities." New York, May, <www.mckinsey.com/mgi/publications/sweden/>.

McKinsey Global Institute (2007), "Universal Principles for Health Care Reform." *McKinsey Quarterly,* no 1.

Maddison, Angus (1991), *Dynamic Forces in Capitalist Development : A Long-Run Comparative View.* Oxford: Oxford University Press.

Madelin, Alain (2007), Interviewed by Johnny Munkhammar, May 10th.

Malet, Jaime (2006), "Spain's Economic Performance is Sustainable after all." Horsham, UK: Eurointelligence Advicers Ltd, December 15th,
<www.eurointelligence.com/Article3.1018+M573475b5e4f.0.html>.

Merlevede, Bruno & Schoors, Koen (2005), "On the Speed of Economic Reform : Tale of the Tortoise and the Hare." Helsingfors: Bank of Finland/Institute for Economies in Transition (BOFIT Discussion Papers 11), <http://swopec.hhs.se/bofitp/abs/bofitp2005_011.htm>.

Micklethwait, John & Woolridge, Adrian (2005), *The Right Nation—Conservative Power in America.* New York: Penguin Press.

Mitchell, Daniel J (2004), "The Economics of Tax Competition : Harmonization vs Liberalization," in *2004 Index of Economic Freedom.* Washington, DC: The Heritage Foundation and Wall Street Journal.

Mitchell, Daniel J (2007), "Flat World, Flat Taxes," *The American,* April 27th.

Miklos, Ivan (2007), Interviewed by Johnny Munkhammar, May 14th.

Montesquieu (1748), Charles-Louis de Secondat, Baron de La Brède et de Montesquieu, *The Spirit of the Laws.* Kitchener, Ont: Batoche, 2001. Can be accessed through IDEAS, History of Economic Thought Books, McMaster University Archive for the History of Economic Thought.

Munkhammar, Johnny (2005), *European Dawn : After the Social Model.* Stockholm: Timbro/Stockholm Network.

Murphy, Kevin M, Shleifer, Andrei & Vishny, Robert W (1993), "Why Is Rent-Seeking So Costly to Growth?" *The American Economic Review,* vol 83, no 2, May.

Möller, Tommy (2001), *Att lyckas med välfärdsreformer : erfarenheter, strategier och förutsättningar.* Stockholm: Reforminsititutet.

National Center for Public Policy Research (2007), *Shattered Dreams : One Hundred Stories of Government Abuse.* Washington, DC: <www.nationalcenter.org/ShatteredDreams.pdf>.

National Intelligence Council (2004), Mapping the Global Future : Report of the National Intelligence Council's 2020 Project. A Report Based on Consultations With Nongovernmental Experts Around the World. Washington, DC, December, <http://www.dni.gov/nic/NIC_2020_project.html>.

Newsweek (2006), "The Complete List : The Top 100 Global Universities." August 13th, <http://www.msnbc.msn.com/id/14321230/>.

Nicoletti, Giuseppe & Scarpetta, Stefano (2005), "Product Market Reforms and Employment in OECD countries." Paris: Organisation for Economic Cooperation and Development (OECD Economics Department Working Paper 472), <www.oecd.org/LongAbstract/0,2546,en_2649_34833_35878806_119684_1_1_1,00.html>.

Noland, Marcus (2003), "Religion, Culture and Economic Perform-ance." Washington, DC: Institute of International Economics, November 20th, (KDI School of Pub Policy & Management Paper 03–13). Available at SSRN, <http://ssrn.com/abstract=497702>.

Norberg, Johan (2003), *In Defense of Global Capitalism.* Washington, DC: Cato Institute.

Norberg, Johan (2006), *När människan skapade världen.* Stockholm: Timbro.

Nordhaus, William D (1997), "Do Real Output and Real-Wage Measures Capture Reality? : The History of Lighting Suggests Not," in Timothy F Bresnahan & Robert J Gordon (eds), *The Economics of New Goods.* Chicago: University of Chicago Press.

Normann, Göran & Stein, Peter (2006), "Reformer i Europa." Stockholm: Confederation of Swedish Enterprise.

Norton, Andrew (2005), "The Politics of Industrial Relations Reform," *Policy*, vol 21, no 2, Winter.

Oddsson, David (2004), "Iceland's Economic Performance." Address at the American Enterprise Institute, June 15th. Reykjavik: Prime Minister's Office, <http://eng.forsaetisraduneyti.is/minister/speeches-and-articles/nr/1391>.

OECD (2004a), *OECD Key Environmental Indicators.* Paris: Organisation for Economic Cooperation and Development, <www.oecd.org/dataoecd/32/20/31558547.pdf>.

OECD (2004b), *OECD Employment Outlook 2004.* Paris: Organisation for Economic Cooperation and Development, <http://miranda.sourceoecd.org/upload/8104121e.pdf>.

OECD (2005), *OECD Economic Outlook : September.* Paris: Organisation for Economic Cooperation and Development.

OECD (2006a), "Boosting Jobs and Incomes : Policy Lessons from Reassessing the OECD Jobs Strategy." Paris: Organisation for Economic Cooperation and Development, June 15–16, <www.oecd.org/document/56/0,2340,en_2649_201185_36998072_1_1_1_1,00.html>.

OECD (2006b), "Competition In the Provision of Hospital Services." Paris: Organisation for Economic Cooperation and Development/ Directorate for Financial and Enterprise Affairs, (Competition Committee), October 27th, <www.oecd.org/LongAbstract/0,3425,en_2649_34685_37981548_119814_1_1_1,00.html>.

OECD (2006c), *Live Longer, Work Longer : A Synthesis Report.* Paris: Organisation for Economic Cooperation and Development (OECD Aging and Employment Policies), <www.oecd.org/document/ 42/0,3343,en_2649_34747_36104426_1_1_1_1,00.html>.

OECD (2006d), *Denmark.* Paris: Organisation for Economic Cooperation and Development (OECD Economic Surveys).

OECD (2006e), *OECD Reviews of Health Systems – Switzerland.* Paris: Organisation for Economic Cooperation and Development.

OECD (2007a), *Economic Policy Reforms : Going for Growth 2007.* Paris: Organisation for Economic Cooperation and Development, <www.oecd.org/document/8/0,2340,en_2649_201185_37882632_1_ 1_1_1,00.html>.

OECD (2007b), *OECD Factbook 2007 : Economic, Environmental and Social Statistics.* Paris: Organisation for Economic Cooperation and Development, <http://titania.sourceoecd.org/vl=1574395/cl=33/ nw=1/rpsv/factbook/>.

OECD (2007c), "Unit Labour Costs : Annual Indicators." Paris: Organisation for Economic Cooperation and Development (OECD Statistics), <http://stats.oecd.org/ WBOS/default.aspx?DatasetCode=ULC_ANN>.

OECD (2007d), *Revenue Statistics 1965–2006.* Paris: Organisation for Economic Cooperation and Development, <www.oecd.org/ document/58/0,3343,en_2649_201185_39498298_1_1_1_1,00.html>.

OECD (2007e), Statistics assembled from "OECD Statistics v.4.4." Paris: Organisation for Economic Cooperation and Development, <http://stats.oecd.org/wbos/default.aspx>.

OECD Observer (2006), "Wealthy Fun." May, <www.oecdobserver.org/news/fullstory.php/aid/1853/ Wealthy_fun.html>.

OECD Statistical Database (2000), "Taxation of Wage Income." Paris: Organisation for Economic Cooperation and Development, <www.oecd.org/dataoecd/44/0/1942482.xls>.

Olofsgård, Anders (2003), "The Political Economy of Reform : Institutional Change as a Tool for Political Credibility." Washington, Georgetown University/Edmund A Walsh School of Foreign Service, December 4th (Background Report to the 2005 World Development Report), <http://siteresources.worldbank.org/INTWDR2005/ Resources/wdr2005_olofsgard_political_economy.pdf>.

Olson, Mancur (1982), *The Rise and Decline of Nations.* New Haven: Yale University Press.

O'Neill, June E & Hill, M Anne (2001), *Gaining Ground? Measuring the Impact of Welfare Reform on Welfare and Work.* New York: Manhattan Institute for Policy Research (Civic Report 17).

Open Europe (2007), "Poll on the Future of Europe : Main Findings Report." London, March 23rd, <www.openeurope.org.uk/research/mainfindings.pdf>.

Özenen, Cem Galip (2006), "The Effects of Structural Funds on Ireland's Development and Lessons For Turkey." Ankara: T R Prime Ministry/State Planning Organization, May, <http://ekutup.dpt.gov.tr/ab/ozenencg/irlanda.pdf>.

Palme, Mårten, Sundén, Annika & Söderlind, Paul (2005), "Investment Choice In the Swedish Premium Pension Plan." Boston: Center for Retirement Research at Boston College, (CRR Working Paper 2005–06).

Persson, Torsten & Tabellini, Guido (1998), "The Size and Scope of Government : Comparative Politics With Rational Politicians." Cambridge, MA: National Bureau of Economic Research, December (NBER Working Paper 6848).

The Pew Research Center (2007a), "A Portrait of "Generation Next" : How Young People View Their Lives, Futures and Politics." Washington, DC, January 9th, <http://people-press.org/reports/display.php3?ReportID=300>.

The Pew Research Center (2007b), "Global Unease With Major World Powers." Washington, DC, June 27th (The Pew Global Attitudes Project), <http://pewglobal.org/reports/pdf/256.pdf>.

Phelps, Edmund S (1997), "A Strategy for Employment and Growth : The Failure of Statism, Welfarism and Free Markets." *Rivista Italiana Degli Economisti*, vol 2, no 1, April.

Phelps, Edmund S (2007a), "Entrepreneurial Culture." *Wall Street Journal*, February 12th.

Phelps, Edmund S (2007b), Lecture at the Conference "Going for Growth" in Almedalen, July 9th. Stockholm: Confederation of Swedish Enterprise.

Pirie, Madsen (1988), *Privatization*. Aldershot: Wildwood House Limited.

Pitney Jr, John J (2000), *The Art of Political Warfar.* Norman, OK: University of Oklahoma Press.

Posen, Adam S (2005a), "Will an Economic Upswing + Elections = Reform?" *European Economic Outlook.* Washington, DC: Peter G Peterson Institute for International Economics, IIE, September 14th.

Posen, Adam S (2005b), "What Is Needed to Make Reforms Work?" *Handelsblatt*, August 19th.

Putnam, Robert D (2000), *Bowling Alone : The Collapse and Revival of American Community.* New York: Simon & Schuster.

Rae, David, Vogt, Line & Wise, Michael (2006), "Boosting Competition in Ireland." Paris: Organization for Economic Cooperation and Development (OECD Economics Department Working Paper 491).

Reding, Viviane (2006), "The Review 2006 of EU Telecom rules : Strengthening Competition and Completing the Internal Market." Annual Meeting of BITKOM. Brussels: Bibliothèque Solvay, June 27th, <http://europa.eu/rapid/pressReleasesAction.do?reference=SPEECH/06/422>.

Rhodes, Martin (2001), "The Political Economy of Social Pacts : 'Competitive Corporatism' and European Welfare reform," in Paul Pierson, ed, *The New Politics of the Welfare State.* Oxford/New York: Oxford University Press.

Riches-Flores, Véronique (2007), "European Competitiveness in the Face of Globalization." Address at Global Insight's World Economic Outlook Conference, May 9–10, in Paris. Paris: Global Insight, May 9th.

Rodrik, Dani (1996), "Understanding Economic Policy Reform." *Journal of Economic Literature*, vol 34 (March).

Rojas, Mauricio (2003), *The Sorrows of Carmencita.* Stockholm: Timbro.

Rosenberg, Nathan & Birdzell, Jr, L E (1986), *How the West Grew Rich.* New York: Basic Books.

Saatchi, Maurice (2005), "Saatchi: Why Tories Lost the Election." BBC News June 20th.

Sacconi, Maurizio (2007), Interviewed by Johnny Munkhammar, May 8th.

Saint-Paul, Gilles (1993), "On the Political Economy of Labour Market Flexibility." London: Centre for Economic Policy Research, August (CEPR Discussion Paper 803).

Saint-Paul, Gilles, Bean, Charles R & Bertola, Giuseppe (1996), "Exploring the Political Economy of Labour Market Institutions." Economic Policy, vol 11, no 23, October.

Saint-Paul, Gilles (1998), "Assessing the Political Viability of Labour Market Reform : The Case of Employment Protection." Barcelona: Universitat Pompeu Fabra/CEPR, December 9th (Working Paper 346).

Saltman, Richard B & Figueras, Josep, eds (1997), "European Health Care Reform : Analysis of Current Strategies." Brussels: European Observatory on Health Systems and Policies.

Sánches-Mier, Luis (2005), "A Theory of Political Influence and Economic Organization." Guanajuato, Mexico: Universidad de Guanajuato/Escuela de Economía, January. Downloadable from <http://ideas.repec.org/p/gua/wpaper/ec200504.html>.

Sandström, Mikael F (2002), *Rätt att välja : hur konkurrens leder till bättre skolor.* Stockholm: Timbro/Centrum för välfärd efter välfärdsstaten.

Sandström, F Mikael & Bergström, Fredrik (2002), "School Vouchers In Practice : Competition Won't Hurt You!" Stockholm: The Research Institute of Industrial Economics, IUI (Working Paper 578).

Sapir, André (2003), *An Agenda for a Growing Europe : Making the EU Economic System Deliver.* Report of an Independent High-Level Study Group established on the initiative of the President of the European Commission. Brussels: The European Commission, July.

Schenström, Ulrica (2007), Interviewed by Johnny Munkhammar, May 22nd.

Schuknecht, Ludger & Tanzi, Vito (2005), "Reforming Public Expenditure in Industrialised Countries : Are There Trade-Offs?" Frankfurt am Main: European Central Bank, February (Working Paper 435).

Schumpeter, Joseph (1975), *Capitalism, Socialism and Democracy.* New York: Harper & Row.

Segerfeldt, Fredrik (2005), *Water for Sale.* Washington, Dc: Cato Institute.

Skousen, Mark (2001), The Making of Modern Economics. Armonk, NY: M E Sharpe.

Sosvilla-Rivero, Simón (2005), "EU Structural Funds and Spain's Objective 1 Regions : An Analysis Based on the Hermin Model." Madrid: Fundación de Estudios de Economía Aplicada, October (FEDEA Working Paper 2005-24).

Stein, Gabriel & Reading, Brian (2003), "Baby Boomer's Poverty Trap : Continental/Japanese Aging." *Monthly International Review,* September (Lombard Street Research).

The Stockholm Network (2007), "Network Map." London, <www.stockholm-network.org/network/map.php>.

Stockholms-Tidningen (1983), Photo of former Finance Minster, Kjell-Olof Feldt, writing down his comment on the Swedish löntagarfonderna. Stockholm, December 20th.

Stone, Debroah (2002), *Policy Paradox : The Art of Political Decision Making.* Rev ed. New York: W W Norton & Company.

Sun Tzu (1991), *The Art of War.* Translated by Thomas Cleary. Boston: Shambhala Pocket Classics.

The Swedish Association of Independent Schools, Website, <http://www.friskola.se/Om_oss_In_English_DXNI-38495_.aspx>.

Tanner, Michael D (2006), "The Critics Were Wrong." *San Francisco Chronicle,* August 21st.

Tanzi, Vito & Schuknecht, Ludger (1996), "Reforming Government in Industrial Countries." *Finance and Development,* September, <www.imf.org/external/pubs/ft/fandd/1996/09/pdf/tanzi.pdf>.

Tanzi, Vito & Schuknecht, Ludger (1997), "Reconsidering the Fiscal Role of Government : The International Perspective." *The American Economic Review,* vol 87, no 2, May.

Teather, Richard (2005), *The Benefits of Tax Competition.* London: The Institute of Economic Affairs.

Thatcher, Margaret (1993), *The Downing Street Years.* London: Harper Collins.

The Times Higher Education Supplement (2007), "World University Rankings." London: *Times,* <www.thes.co.uk/worldrankings/>.

Tiraboschi, Michele (2006a), "Young People and Employment in Italy : The (Difficult) Transition From Education and Training to the Labour Market." *International Journal of Comparative Labour Law & Industrial Relations,* Spring.

Tiraboschi, Michele (2006b), "The Italian Labour Market After the Biagi Reform." Modena, Italy: University of Modena and Reggio Emilia, 2006, <www.csmb.unimo.it/index/other/Journal.pdf>.

Tridimas, George & Winer, Stanley L (2005), "The Political Economy of Government Size." *European Journal of Political Economy,* vol 21, no 3, September.

Trotter, Ron, Sir (1996), "From Basket Case To Case Study : New Zealand 1984–96." Wellington: New Zealand Business Round Table, <www.nzbr.org.nz/documents/speeches/speeches-96-97/trotter-speech.pdf>.

True, James L, Jones, Bryan D & Baumgartner, Frank R (1999), "Punctuated-Equilibrium Theory : Explaining Stability and Change in Public Policymaking," in Paul A Sabatier, ed, *Theories of the Policy Process.* Boulder, CO/Oxford: Westview.

Tulip, Peter (2007), "Financial Markets in Iceland." Paris: Organisation for Economic Cooperation and Development (OECD Economics Department Working Paper 549).

Tullock, Gordon (2006), *The Vote Motive.* London: The Institute of Economic Affairs (first published in 1976).

Tversky, Amos (1990), "The Psychology of Risk," in Ambachtsheer, Keith P, et al, *Quantifying the Risk Premium Phenomena For Investment decision Making.* Charlottesville, VA: The Institute of Chartered Financial Analysts.

Uddhammar, Emil (1993), *Partierna och den stora staten.* Stockholm: City University Press.

UNDP (2006), *Human Development Report 2007/2008 : Fighting climate Change.* New York: United Nations Development Programme, <http://hdr.undp.org/>.

United Nations (2006), "World Population Prospects : The 2006 Revision." New York, <http://esa.un.org/unpp/>.

Velfærdskommissionen (2005), *Fremtidens velfærd : vores valg.* Copenhagen, December, <www.velfaerd.dk/>.

Veenhoven, Ruut (1997), "Quality of Life in Individualistic Society : A Comparison of 43 Nations in the Early 1990s," in M J deJong & A C Zijderveld (eds), *The Gift of Society.* Nijker, The Netherlands: Enzo Press.

Wasmer, Etienne (2006), "The Economics of Prozac : Do Employees Really Gain From Strong Unemployment Protection?" Paris: Institut d'Études Politiques de Paris/OFCE/CEPR/IZA, November (IZA Discussion Paper 2460).

Weber, Max (2002), *The Protestant Ethic and the "Spirit" of Capitalism and Other Writings.* New York: Penguin Books (first published 1905).

Welch, Jack & Welch, Suzy (2005), *Winning.* New York: Harper Collins.

Westerberg, Bengt (2000), "Har vi råd med äldrevård när 40-talisterna blir gamla?" Stockholm: Pensionsforum, <www.pensionsforum.nu/westerberg.pdf>.

Williamson, John, ed (1994), *The Political Economy of Policy Reform.* Washington, DC: Institute for International Economics.

Williamson, John & Haggard, Stephen (1994), "The Political Conditions for Economic Reform," in John Williamson, ed, *The Political Economy of Policy Reform.* Washington, DC: Institute of International Economics.

The World Bank (2006a), *Paying Taxes : the Global Picture.* Washington, DC: The World Bank/Price Waterhouse Coopers.

The World Bank (2006b), *World Development Indicators 2006.* Washington, DC (WDI Online), <http://web.worldbank.org/WBSITE/EXTERNAL/DATASTATISTICS/0,,contentMDK:20899413~pagePK:64133150~piPK:64133175~theSitePK:239419,00.html>.

The World Bank (2007a), *World Development Indicators 2007.* Washington, DC, <http://publications.worldbank.org/ecommerce/catalog/product?item_id=6355166>.

The World Bank (2007b), *World Development Report 1978–2007.* Washington, DC.

World Database of Happiness, Website, Directed by Ruut Veenhoven. Rotterdam: Erasmus University, <http://worlddatabaseofhappiness.eur.nl/>.

World Economic Forum (2007), *Global Competitiveness Report.* Geneva, <www.weforum.org/en/initiatives/gcp/Global %20Competitiveness%20Report/GlobalCompetitivnessReport>.

World Health Organization (a), "World Health Chart." Geneva, <www.whc.ki.se>.

World Health Organization (b), "Life Tables for WHO Members." Geneva, <http://www.who.int/ whosis/database/life_tables/life_tables.cfm>.

Wykoff, Frank C (2001), "Creating Capitalism : Politics, Reforms and Economic Performance." Claremont, CA: Claremont Colleges (Working Paper 2001-17).

Yergin, Daniel & Stanislaw, Joseph (1998), *Commanding Heights : The Battle Between Government and the Marketplace That Is Remaking the Modern World.* New York: Simon & Schuster.

Zee, Howell H (1996), "Fiscal Policy and Long-Run Growth." Washington, DC: International Monetary Fund, October (IMF Working Paper 96/119).

Zsiga, Erik, *Bye, Bye, Eastern Europe.* Forthcoming.

Zwinkels, Wim, Brouwer, Peter & Braat, Adriaan (2006), "Verzekerd van een effectieve prikkel." Hoofddorp, NL: TNO Kwaliteit van Leven, May 30th (TNO Report 22083/11381).

ABOUT THE AUTHOR

JOHNNY MUNKHAMMAR (b. 1974) is an analyst and commentator specialising in political and economic affairs, more specifically free-market reforms, globalisation, labour markets, European integration and foreign policy. He is affiliated with several think-tanks and policy institutes in Europe and the United States, including Timbro, the Centre for European Policy Analysis and European Enterprise Institute.

Mr. Munkhammar holds a Master's Degree from Uppsala University, Sweden, where he majored in political science and minored in economics and economic history.

European Dawn is the most recent of Mr. Munkhammar's five books. He has additionally contributed to numerous books, including *2007 Index of Economic Freedom,* as well as to a range of studies and policy papers.

Mr. Munkhammar is a member of several societies and networks that engage in international economic and political matters. He is a sought-after speaker and panellist, appearing at conferences, corporations, institutes and universities across Europe and the United States.

Previously, Mr. Munkhammar served as a senior adviser at the Confederation of Swedish Enterprise, leader writer at several local daily newspapers in Sweden, as well as a partner at a public affairs firm.

A frequent commentator and contributor to broadcast and print media, Mr. Munkhammar has also published hundreds of op-eds in leading international publications.

Mr. Munkhammar resides in Stockholm, Sweden, with his wife and daughter.

For further details, please visit www.munkhammar.org